# The Cognitive Style of PowerPoint: Pitching Out Corrupts Within

IN corporate and government bureaucracies, the standard method for making a presentation is to talk about a list of points organized onto stylized slides projected up on the wall. For years, before computerized presentations, those giving a talk used transparencies for projected images. Now presenters use a slideware program, Microsoft PowerPoint, which turns out billions and billions of presentation slides each year.

This chapter provides evidence that *compares PowerPoint with alternative methods for presenting information*: 10 case studies, an unbiased collection of 2,000 PP slides, and 32 control samples from non-PP presentations.

The evidence indicates that PowerPoint, compared to other common presentation tools, reduces the analytical quality of serious presentations of evidence. This is especially the case for the PowerPoint ready-made templates, which corrupt statistical reasoning, and often weaken verbal and spatial thinking. What is the problem with PowerPoint? And more importantly, how can we improve our presentations?

WHEN Louis Gerstner became president of IBM, he encountered a big company caught up in ritualistic slideware-style presentations:

> One of the first meetings I asked for was briefing on the state of the [mainframe computer] business. I remember at least two things about that first meeting with Nick Donofrio, who was then running the System/390 business . . . .

> At that time, the standard format of any important IBM meeting was a presentation using overhead projectors and graphics that IBMers called "foils" [projected transparencies]. Nick was on his second foil when I stepped to the table and, as politely as I could in front of his team, switched off the projector. After a long moment of awkward silence, I simply said, "Let's just talk about your business."

> I mention this episode because it had an unintended, but terribly powerful ripple effect. By that afternoon an email about my hitting the Off button on the overhead projector was crisscrossing the world. Talk about consternation! It was as if the President of the United States had banned the use of English at White House meetings.[1]

[1] Louis V. Gerstner, Jr., *Who Says Elephants Can't Dance? Inside IBM's Historic Turnaround* (2002), 43.

4

## *The Cognitive Style of PowerPoint*

GERSTNER'S blunt action shutting down the projector suggests that there are better tools for doing business analysis than reading aloud from bullet lists: "*Let's just talk about your business.*" Indeed, Gerstner later asked IBM executives to write out their business strategies in longhand using the presentation methodology of *sentences*, with subjects and predicates, nouns and verbs, which then combine sequentially to form *paragraphs*, an analytic tool demonstratively better than slideware bullet lists.[2]

[2] Gordon Shaw, Robert Brown, Philip Bromiley, "Strategic Stories: How 3M is Rewriting Business Planning," *Harvard Business Review*, 76 (May-June, 1998), 42-44.

"*Let's just talk about your business*" indicates a thoughtful exchange of information, a mutual interplay between speaker and audience, rather than a pitch made by a power pointer pointing to bullets. PowerPoint is *presenter-oriented, not content-oriented, not audience-oriented.* PP advertising is not about content quality, but rather presenter therapy: "A cure for the presentation jitters." "Get yourself organized." "Use the AutoContent Wizard to figure out what you want to say."

PowerPoint's convenience for some presenters is costly to the content and the audience. These costs arise from the *cognitive style characteristic of the standard default PP presentation:* foreshortening of evidence and thought, low spatial resolution, an intensely hierarchical single-path structure as the model for organizing every type of content, breaking up narratives and data into slides and minimal fragments, rapid temporal sequencing of thin information rather than focused spatial analysis, conspicuous chartjunk and PP Phluff, branding of slides with logotypes, a preoccupation with format not content, incompetent designs for data graphics and tables, and a smirky commercialism that turns information into a sales pitch and presenters into marketeers.

PowerPoint comes with a big attitude. Other than video games, not many computer programs have attitudes. Effective tools such as web browsers, Word, Excel, Photoshop, and Illustrator are not accompanied by distinctive cognitive styles that reduce the intellectual level of the content passing through the program.

Nonetheless, PowerPoint may benefit the bottom 10% of all presenters. PP forces them to have *points*, some points, any points. Slideware perhaps helps inept speakers get their act together, outline talks, retrieve visual materials, present slides. Furthermore, PP probably doesn't cause much damage to really first-rate presenters, say the top 10%, who have strong content, self-awareness, and their own analytical style that avoids or neutralizes the PP style. This leaves 80%, workaday presenters for whom the PP cognitive style may cause trouble, especially for those seeking to present evidence and serious analysis.

In practice, PP slides are very low resolution compared to paper, many computer screens, and the immense visual capacities of the human eye-brain system. With little information per slide, many many slides are needed. Audiences endure a relentless sequentiality, one damn slide after another. Information stacked in time makes it difficult to understand context and evaluate relationships. Visual reasoning usually works more effectively when the relevant evidence is shown *adjacent in space* within our eyespan. This is especially the case for statistical data, where the fundamental analytical task is to make comparisons.

The statistical graphics produced by PowerPoint are astonishingly thin, nearly content-free. In 28 books on PP templates, the 217 model statistical graphics depict an average of 12 numbers each (as do the PP data table templates). Compared to the worldwide publications shown here, the PP statistical graphics are the thinnest of all, except for those in *Pravda* in 1982, back when that newspaper operated as the major propaganda instrument of the Soviet communist party and a totalitarian government.[3] Doing a bit better than *Pravda* is not good enough:

MEDIAN NUMBER OF ENTRIES IN DATA MATRICES FOR
STATISTICAL GRAPHICS IN VARIOUS PUBLICATIONS, 2003

| | |
|---|---|
| *Science* | > 1,000 |
| *Nature* | > 700 |
| *New York Times* | 120 |
| *Wall Street Journal* | 112 |
| *Frankfurter Allgemeine Zeitung* | 98 |
| *New England Journal of Medicine* | 53 |
| *Asahi* | 40 |
| *Financial Times* | 40 |
| *The Economist* | 32 |
| *Le Monde* | 28 |
| 28 books on PowerPoint presentations (1997–2003) | 12 |
| *Pravda* (1982) | 5 |

These PP graph templates are particularly unfortunate for students, since for all too many their *first* experience in presenting statistical evidence is via PP designs, which create the impression that data graphics are for propaganda and advertisements not for reasoning about information.

And, in presenting *words*, impoverished space encourages imprecise statements, slogans, abrupt and thinly-argued claims. For example, this slide from a statistics course shows a seriously incomplete cliché. In fact, probably the *shortest true statement* that can be made about causality and correlation is "*Empirically observed covariation is a necessary but not sufficient condition for causality.*" Or perhaps "*Correlation is not causation but it sure is a hint.*" Many true statements are too long to fit on a PP slide, but this does not mean we should abbreviate the truth to make the words fit. It means we should find a better tool to make presentations.

[3] In this table, the medians are based on at least 20 statistical graphics and at least one full issue of each publication. These publications, except for scientific journals, tend to use the same graph designs issue after issue; thus replications of several of the counts were within 10% of the original result. Data for other publications (*Pravda*, for example) are reported in Edward R. Tufte, *The Visual Display of Quantitative Information* (1983, 2001), 167.

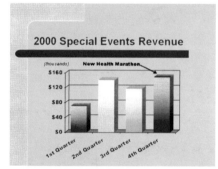

*Pravda*, May 24, 1982.

## Sequentiality of the Slide Format

WITH information quickly appearing and disappearing, the slide transition is an event that attracts attention to the presentation's compositional methods. Slide serve up a small chunks of promptly vanishing information in a restless one-way sequence. It is not a contemplative analytical method; it is like television, or a movie with over-frequent random jump cuts. Sometimes quick chunks of thin data may be useful (flash-card memorizing), other times not (comparisons, links, explanations). *But formats, sequencing, and cognitive approach should be decided by the character of the content and what is to be explained, not by the limitations of the presentation technology.* The talk that accompanies PP slides may overcome the noise and clutter that results from slideville's arbitrary partitioning of data, but why disrupt the signal in the first place? And why should we need to recover from a technology that is supposed to help our presentations?

Obnoxious transitions and partitions occur not only slide-by-slide but also line-by-line, as in the dreaded slow reveal (at right). Beginning with a title slide, the presenter unveils and reads aloud the single line on the slide, then reveals the next line, reads that aloud, on and on, as the stupefied audience impatiently awaits the end of the talk.

It is helpful to provide audience members with at least one mode of information that allows *them* to control the order and pace of learning—unlike slides and unlike talk. Paper handouts for talks will help provide a permanent record for review—again unlike projected images and talk. Another way to break free of low-resolution temporal comparisons is to show multiple slides, several images at once within the common view. Spatial parallelism takes advantage of our notable capacity to reason about multiple images that appear simultaneously within our eyespan. We are able to select, sort, edit, reconnoiter, review—ways of seeing quickened and sharpened by direct spatial adjacency of evidence.

Now and then the narrow bandwidth and relentless sequencing of PP slides are said to be virtues, a claim justified by loose reference to George Miller's classic 1956 paper "The Magical Number Seven, Plus or Minus Two." That essay reviews psychological experiments that discovered people had a hard time remembering more than about 7 unrelated pieces of really dull data all at once. These studies on memorizing nonsense then led some interface designers, as well as PP guideline writers seeking to make a virtue of a necessity, to conclude that only 7 items belong on a list or a slide, a conclusion that can only be reached by not reading Miller's paper. In fact the paper neither states nor implies rules for the amount of information shown on a slide (except for those presentations consisting of nonsense syllables that the audience must memorize and repeat back to a psychologist). On the contrary, the deep point of Miller's work is to suggest strategies, such as placing evidence within a context, that extend the reach of memory beyond tiny clumps of data.[4]

The Dreaded Build Sequence

The Dreaded Build Sequence
THE FIRST LINE IS REVEALED

The Dreaded Build Sequence
THE FIRST LINE IS REVEALED
THE SECOND LINE IS REVEALED!

The Dreaded Build Sequence
THE FIRST LINE IS REVEALED
THE SECOND LINE IS REVEALED!
THE THIRD LINE IS REVEALED

[THE AUDIENCE FLEES]

[4] George A. Miller, "The Magical Number Seven, Plus or Minus Two: Some Limits on Our Capacity for Processing Information," *Psychological Review*, 63 (1956), 81-97 (and widely posted on the internet). At Williams College in September 2000, I saw George Miller give a presentation that used the optimal number of bullet points on the optimal number of slides—zero in both cases. Just a straightforward talk with a long narrative structure.

*Metaphors for Presentations*

THE metaphor of PowerPoint is *the software corporation itself*. To describe a software house is to describe the PP cognitive style: a big bureaucracy engaged in *computer programming* (deep hierarchical structures, relentlessly sequential, nested, one-short-line-at-a-time) and in *marketing* (advocacy not analysis, more style than substance, misdirection, slogan thinking, fast pace, branding, exaggerated claims, marketplace ethics). That the PP cognitive style mimics a software house exemplifies *Conway's Law:*

> Any organization which designs a system . . . will inevitably produce a design whose structure is a copy of the organization's communication structure.[5]

Why should the structure, activities, and values of a large commercial bureaucracy be a useful metaphor for our presentations? Are there worse metaphors? Voice-mail menu systems? Billboards? Television? Stalin?

The pushy PP style imposes itself on the audience and tends to set up a dominance relationship between speaker and audience. Too often the speaker is making *power points with hierarchical bullets to passive followers*. Aggressive, stereotyped, over-managed presentations—the Great Leader up on the pedestal—are characteristic of hegemonic systems:

> The Roman state bolstered its authority and legitimacy with the trappings of ceremony. . . . Power is a far more complex and mysterious quality than any apparently simple manifestation of it would appear. It is as much a matter of impression, of theatre, of persuading those over whom authority is wielded to collude in their subjugation. Insofar as power is a matter of presentation, its cultural currency in antiquity (and still today) was the creation, manipulation, and display of images. In the propagation of the imperial office, at any rate, art was power.[6]

A BETTER metaphor for presentations is *good teaching*. Practical teaching techniques are very useful for presentations in general. Teachers seek to explain something with credibility, which is what many presentations are trying to do. The core ideas of teaching—*explanation, reasoning, finding things out, questioning, content, evidence, credible authority not patronizing authoritarianism*—are contrary to the cognitive style of PowerPoint. And the ethical values of teachers differ from those engaged in marketing.[7]

Especially disturbing is the introduction of PowerPoint into schools. Instead of writing a report using sentences, children learn how to decorate client pitches and infomercials, which is better than encouraging children to smoke. Student PP exercises (as seen in teacher's guides, and in student work posted on the internet) typically show 5 to 20 words and a piece of clip art on each slide in a presentation consisting of 3 to 6 slides—a total of perhaps 80 words (20 seconds of silent reading) for a week of work. Rather than being trained as mini-bureaucrats in the pitch culture, students would be better off if schools closed down on PP days and everyone went to The Exploratorium. Or wrote an illustrated essay explaining something.

[5] Melvin E. Conway, "How Do Committees Invent?," *Datamation*, April 1968, 28–31. The law's "inevitably" overreaches. Frederick P. Brooks, Jr., in *The Mythical Man-Month: Essays on Software Engineering* (1975), famously describes the interplay between system design and bureaucracy.

[6] Jás Elsner, *Imperial Rome and Christian Triumph: The Art of the Roman Empire AD 100-450* (1998), 53.

[7] On teaching and presentations: Joseph Lowman, *Mastering the Techniques of Teaching* (1995); Wilbert J. McKeachie and Barbara K. Hofer, *McKeachie's Teaching Tips* (2001); Frederick Mosteller, "Classroom and Platform Performance," *The American Statistician*, 34 (February 1980), 11–17 (also posted on internet).

*PowerPoint Does Rocket Science: Assessing the Quality and Credibility of Technical Reports*

NEARLY all engineering presentations at NASA are made in PowerPoint.
Is this a product endorsement or a big mistake? Does PP's cognitive
style affect the quality of engineering analysis? How does PP compare
with alternative methods of technical presentation? Some answers come
from the evidence of NASA PowerPoint in action: (1) hundreds of PP
technical presentations experienced in 2003 by the Columbia Accident
Investigation Board and in 2005 by the Return to Flight Task Group,
(2) a case study of the PP presentations for NASA officials making life-
and-death decisions during the final flight of Columbia, (3) observations
by Richard Feynman who saw a lot of slideware-style presentations in
his NASA work on the 1986 Challenger accident, (4) my observations as
a NASA consultant on technical presentations for shuttle risk assessments,
shuttle engineering, and deep spaceflight trajectories.

DURING the January 2003 spaceflight of shuttle Columbia, 82 seconds
after liftoff, a 1.67 pound (760 grams) piece of foam insulation broke
off from the liquid fuel tank, hit the left wing, and broke through the
wing's thermal protection. After orbiting the Earth for 2 weeks with an
undetected hole in its wing, the Columbia burned up during re-entry
because the compromised thermal protection was unable to withstand
the intense temperatures that occur upon atmosphere re-entry. The *only*
evidence of a possible problem was a very brief video sequence showing
that something hit the wing somewhere. Here are 2 frame-captures
from a video at 82 seconds after Columbia's launch:

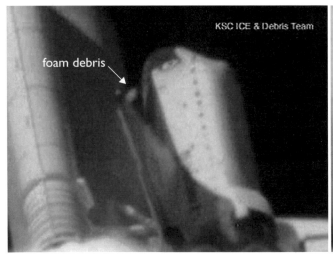 

The rapidly accelerating Columbia in effect ran into the
foam debris. Post-accident frame-by-frame analysis yields
the impact velocity of the foam, 600 miles or 970 km per
hour, the speed of sound. Since kinetic energy = $\frac{1}{2}mv^2$,
the velocity-squared contribution is substantial.

In the video, 2 relevant variables are indeterminate: impact
*angle of incidence* and impact *location*. Did the debris hit the
insulation tiles on the left wing, or the reinforced carbon-
carbon (RCC) on the leading edge of the wing? Post-accident
investigation established that the foam hit the especially
vulnerable RCC.

What to make of this video? How serious is the threat? What actions should be taken in response? A quick, smart analysis is needed, since Columbia will re-enter the atmosphere in about 12 days. Although the evidence is uncertain and thin, for only a single camera showed debris impact, the logical structure of the engineering analysis is straightforward:

| debris *kinetic energy* (function of mass, velocity, and angle of incidence) | + | debris hits locations of *varying vulnerability* on left wing | → | *level of threat* to the Columbia during re-entry heating of wing |

*Angle of incidence* is uncertain; *location of impact* is uncertain (wing tiles? leading edge of the wing?); *mass* and *velocity* of the foam debris can be calculated. Profoundly relevant is the *difference in velocity* between the shuttle and the piece of free-floating foam, since the kinetic energy of the foam impact is proportional to that *velocity squared*. Even though the errant foam was lightweight (1.67 lb), it was moving fast (600 mph) relative to the shuttle. Velocity squared is like shipping and handling: it will get you every time.

To help NASA officials assess the threat, Boeing Corporation engineers quickly prepared 3 reports, a total of 28 PowerPoint slides, dealing with the debris impact.[8] These reports provided mixed readings of the threat to the Columbia; the lower-level bullets often mentioned doubts and uncertainties, but the highlighted executive summaries and big-bullet conclusions were quite optimistic. Convinced that the reports indicated no problem rather than uncertain knowledge, high-level NASA officials decided that the Columbia was safe and, furthermore, that no additional investigations were necessary. Several NASA engineers had hoped that the military would photograph the Columbia with high-resolution spy cameras, which would have easily detected the damage, but even that checkup was thought unnecessary given the optimism of the 3 Boeing reports. And so the Columbia orbited for nearly 2 weeks with a big undetected hole in its wing.

ON the next page, I examine a key slide in the PP reports made while the Columbia was damaged but still flying. The analysis demonstrates methods for how not to get fooled while consuming a presentation. Imagine that you are a high-level NASA decision-maker receiving a pitch about threats to the Columbia. You must learn 2 things: Exactly what is the presenter's story? And, can you *believe* the presenter's story? To assess the quality of intellect and credibility of presenters, close readings of their work will prove revealing. To be effective, close readings must be based on *universal* standards of evidence quality, which are not necessarily those standards operating in Houston that day. Also this reading reveals some shortcomings of PowerPoint for technical work, a point made by several investigations of shuttle engineering practices.

[8] C. Ortiz, A. Green, J. McClymonds, J. Stone, A. Khodadoust, "Preliminary Debris Transport Assessment of Debris Impacting Orbiter Lower Surface in STS-107 Mission," January 21, 2003; P. Parker, D. Chao, I. Norman, M. Dunham, "Orbiter Assessment of STS-107 ET Bipod Insulation Ramp Impact," January 23, 2003; C. Ortiz, "Debris Transport Assessment of Debris Impacting Orbiter Lower Surface in STS-107 Mission," January 24, 2003. These reports were published in records of the CAIB and at NASA websites.

---

**Summary and Conclusion**

- Impact analysis ("Crater") indicates potential for large TPS damage
  - Review of test data shows wide variation in impact response
  - RCC damage limited to coating based on soft SOFI
- Thermal analysis of wing with missing tile is in work
  - Single tile missing shows local structural damage is possible, but no burn through
  - Multiple tile missing analysis is on-going
- M/OD criteria used to assess structural impacts of tile loss
  - Allows significant temperature exceedance, even some burn through
    - Impact to vehicle turnaround possible, but maintains safe return capability

Conclusion
- Contingent on multiple tile loss thermal analysis showing no violation of M/OD criteria, safe return indicated even with significant tile damage

*BOEING*      13

On this one Columbia slide, a PowerPoint festival of bureaucratic hyper-rationalism, 6 different levels of hierarchy are used to display, classify, and arrange 11 phrases:

Level 1     Title of Slide
Level 2     ●   Very Big Bullet
Level 3       —   big dash
Level 4          ◆   medium-small diamond
Level 5             •   tiny bullet
Level 6                 ( )   parentheses ending level 5

The analysis begins with the dreaded Executive Summary, with a conclusion presented as a headline: "Test Data Indicates Conservatism for Tile Penetration." This turns out to be unmerited reassurance. Executives, at least those who don't want to get fooled, had better read far beyond the title.

The "conservatism" concerns the *choice of models* used to predict damage. But why, after 112 flights, are foam-debris models being calibrated during a crisis? How can "conservatism" be inferred from a loose comparison of a spreadsheet model and some thin data? Divergent evidence means divergent evidence, not inferential security. Claims of analytic "conservatism" should be viewed with skepticism by presentation consumers. Such claims are often a rhetorical tactic that substitutes verbal fudge factors for quantitative assessments.

As the bullet points march on, the seemingly reassuring headline fades away. Lower-level bullets at the end of the slide undermine the executive summary. This third-level point notes that "Flight condition [that is, the debris hit on the Columbia] is significantly outside of test database." How far outside? The final bullet will tell us.

This fourth-level bullet concluding the slide reports that the debris hitting the Columbia is estimated to be 1920/3 = 640 times larger than data used in the tests of the model! The correct headline should be "Review of Test Data Indicates Irrelevance of Two Models." This is a powerful conclusion, indicating that pre-launch safety standards no longer hold. The original optimistic headline has been eviscerated by the lower-level bullets. Note how close attentive readings can help consumers of presentations evaluate the presenter's reasoning and credibility.

The Very-Big-Bullet phrase fragment does not seem to make sense. No other VBB's appear in the rest of the slide, so this VBB is not necessary.

Spray On Foam Insulation, a fragment of which caused the hole in the wing

**Review of Test Data Indic**
**Pene**

● **The existing SOFI on tile tes**
**was reviewed along with ST**
  — **Crater overpredicted pe**
   **significantly**
    ◆ **Initial penetration to des**
     • Varies with volume/r
     3cu. In)
    ◆ **Significant energy is re**
    **to penetrate the relative**
     • Test results do show
     and velocity
    ◆ **Conversely, once tile is**
    **significant damage**
     • Minor variations in t
     can cause significan
  — **Flight condition is signif**
    ◆ **Volume of ramp is 1920**

*BOEING*

Here "ramp" refers to foam debris (from the bipod ramp) that hit Columbia. Instead of the cryptic "Volume of ramp," say "estimated volume of foam debris that hit the wing." Such clarifying phrases, which may help upper level executives understand what is going on, are too long to fit on low-resolution bullet outline formats. PP demands a shorthand of acronyms, phrase fragments, clipped jargon, and vague pronoun references in order to get at least some information into the tight format.

A model to estimate damage to
the tiles protecting flat surfaces
of the wing

**es Conservatism for Tile**
**tion**

**lata used to create Crater**
**37 Southwest Research data**
**ration of tile coating**

**bed by normal velocity**
**s of projectile (e.g., 200ft/sec for**

**ed for the softer SOFI particle**
**lard tile coating**
**It( it )is possible at sufficient mass**

**netrated SOFI can cause**

**energy (above penetration level)**
**e damage**
**ntly outside of test database**
**n vs 3 cu in for test**

The vigorous, vaguely quantitative, words "significant" and
"significantly" are used 5 times on this slide, with meanings
ranging from "detectable in a perhaps irrelevant calibration
case study" to "an amount of damage so that everyone dies"
to "a difference of 640-fold." None of the 5 "significants"
refer to "statistical significance;" such wordplay hints that
a formal statistical analysis has been done.

Note the analysis is about *tile* penetration. But what about
RCC penetration? As investigators later demonstrated, the
foam did not hit the tiles on the wing surface, but instead
the delicate reinforced-carbon-carbon (RCC) protecting
the wing leading edge. Alert consumers should carefully
watch how presenters delineate *the scope of their analysis,*
a profound and sometimes decisive matter.

?

Slideville's low resolution and large type generate space-
wasting typographic orphans, lonely words dangling on 4
separate lines:
**Penetration**   **significantly**   3cu. In      and velocity

The really vague pronoun reference "it" refers to *damage
to the left wing,* which ultimately destroyed the Columbia
(although the slide here deals with tile not RCC damage).
Low-resolution presentation formats encourage vague
references because there isn't enough space for specific
and precise phrases.

The same unit of measurement for volume (cubic inches)
is shown in a slightly different way every time
   3cu. In     **1920cu in**     **3 cu in**
rather than in clear and tidy exponential form 1920 in$^3$.
Shakiness in conventions for units of measurement should
always provoke concern, as it does in grading the problem
sets of sophomore engineering students.* PowerPoint is
not good at math and science; here at NASA, engineers are
using a presentation tool that apparently makes it difficult to
write scientific notation. The pitch-style typography of PP
is hopeless for science and engineering, yet this important
analysis relied on PP. Technical articles are not published
in PP; why then should PP be used for serious technical
analysis, such as diagnosing the threat to Columbia?

*The Columbia Accident Investigation Board (final
report, p. 191) referred to this point about units of
measurement: "While such inconsistencies might seem
minor, in highly technical fields like aerospace engineering a misplaced decimal point or mistaken unit of
measurement can easily engender inconsistencies and
inaccuracies." The phrase "mistaken unit of measurement" is an unkind veiled reference to a government
agency that had crashed $250 million of spacecraft
into Mars because of a mix-up between metric and
non-metric units of measurement.

In the reports, *every single text-slide* uses bullet-outlines with 4 to 6 levels of hierarchy. Then another multi-level list, another bureaucracy of bullets, *starts afresh* for a new slide. How is it that each elaborate architecture of thought always fits *exactly* on one slide? The rigid slide-by-slide hierarchies, indifferent to content, slice and dice the evidence into arbitrary compartments, producing an anti-narrative with choppy continuity. Medieval in its preoccupation with hierarchical distinctions, the PowerPoint format signals every bullet's status in 4 or 5 different simultaneous ways: by the order in sequence, extent of indent, size of bullet, style of bullet, and size of type associated with various bullets. This is a lot of insecure format for a simple engineering problem.

The format reflects a common conceptual error in analytic design: information architectures mimic the hierarchical structure of large bureaucracies pitching the information. Conway's Law again. In their report, the Columbia Accident Investigation Board found that the distinctive cognitive style of PowerPoint reinforced the hierarchical filtering and biases of the NASA bureaucracy during the crucial period when the Columbia was damaged but still functioning:

> The Mission Management Team Chair's position in the hierarchy governed what information she would or would not receive. Information was lost as it traveled up the hierarchy. A demoralized Debris Assessment Team did not include a slide about the need for better imagery in their presentation to the Mission Evaluation Room. Their presentation included the Crater analysis, which they reported as incomplete and uncertain. However, the Mission Evaluation Room manager perceived the Boeing analysis as rigorous and quantitative. The choice of headings, arrangement of information, and size of bullets on the key chart served to highlight what management already believed. The uncertainties and assumptions that signaled danger dropped out of the information chain when the Mission Evaluation Room manager condensed the Debris Assessment Team's formal presentation to an informal verbal brief at the Mission Management Team meeting.[9]

[9] Columbia Accident Investigation Board, *Report*, volume 1 (August 2003), 201.

At the same time, lower-level NASA engineers were writing about the possible dangers to the Columbia in several hundred emails, with the Boeing reports in PP format sometimes attached. The text of about 90% of these emails simply used *sentences* sequentially ordered into *paragraphs*; 10% used bullet lists with 2 or 3 levels. These engineers were able to reason about the issues without employing the baroque hierarchical outlines of the original PP pitches. Good for them.

Several of these emails referred to the 3 PP reports as the "Boeing PowerPoint Pitch." The WhatPoint Pitch? The PowerWhat Pitch? The PowerPoint What? *The language, attitude, and presentation tool of the pitch culture had penetrated throughout the NASA organization, even into the most serious technical analysis, the survival of the shuttle.*

The analysis of the key Columbia slide on the preceding pages was posted at my website.[10] Much of this material was then included by the final report of Columbia Accident Investigation Board (CAIB). In a discussion of "Engineering by Viewgraphs," the Board went far beyond my case study of the Columbia slide in these extraordinary remarks about PowerPoint:

> As information gets passed up an organization hierarchy, from people who do analysis to mid-level managers to high-level leadership, key explanations and supporting information are filtered out. In this context, it is easy to understand how a senior manager might read this PowerPoint slide and not realize that it addresses a life-threatening situation.

> At many points during its investigation, the Board was surprised to receive similar presentation slides from NASA officials in place of technical reports. The Board views the endemic use of PowerPoint briefing slides instead of technical papers as an illustration of the problematic methods of technical communication at NASA.[11]

The Board makes an explicit comparison: some tools are better than others for engineering, and technical reports are better than PowerPoint.

THEN, 2 years later, 7 members of the Return to Flight Task Group, a powerful external review group created by NASA to monitor the post-Columbia repairs of the shuttle, had something to say about engineering by PowerPoint. After seeing hundreds of PP decks from NASA and its contractors, the Task Group made direct comparisons of alternative presentation tools for engineering analysis and documentation:

> We also observed that instead of concise engineering reports, decisions and their associated rationale are often contained solely within Microsoft Power-Point charts or emails. The CAIB report (vol. 1, pp. 182 and 191) criticized the use of PowerPoint as an engineering tool, and other professional organizations have also noted the increased use of this presentation software as a substitute for technical reports and other meaningful documentation. PowerPoint (and similar products by other vendors), as a method to provide talking points and present limited data to assembled groups, has its place in the engineering community; however, these presentations should never be allowed to replace, or even supplement, formal documentation.

> Several members of the Task Group noted, as had CAIB before them, that many of the engineering packages brought before formal control boards were documented *only* in PowerPoint presentations. In some instances, requirements are defined in presentations, approved with a cover letter, and never transferred to formal documentation. Similarly, in many instances when data was requested by the Task Group, a PowerPoint presentation would be delivered without supporting engineering documentation. It appears that many young engineers do not understand the need for, or know how to prepare, formal engineering documents such as reports, white papers, or analyses.[12]

[10] "Columbia Evidence—Analysis of Key Slide," March 18, 2003, Ask E.T. forum, www.edwardtufte.com

[11] Columbia Accident Investigation Board, *Report*, vol. 1 (August 2003), 191.

[12] Dan L. Crippen, Charles C. Daniel, Amy K. Donahue, Susan J. Helms, Susan Morrisey Livingstone, Rosemary O'Leary, and William Wegner, "A.2, Observations" in *Final Report of the Return to Flight Task Group* (July 2005), 190.

The Return to Flight Task Group made their evaluations and decisions based on closure packages that described the post-Columbia shuttle repairs. In the final report, 7 Task Group members reported that these "inadequate and disorganized" packages, often huge decks of PP slides, provoked "our frustration":[13]

> Closure packages, which should have represented the auditable, documented status of the NASA implementation of the CAIB recommendations, tended to rely on mass, rather than accuracy, as proof of closure. The closure packages showed an organization that apparently still believes PowerPoint presentations adequately explain work and document accomplishments.[14]

In an example of the pitch culture in action, some closure packages were provided prematurely to the Return to Flight Task Group in apparent behind-the-scenes maneuvers to discover just what it might take to get approval for the post-accident shuttle repairs. The idea might have been that if it is too late to change the engineering, then change the pitch about the engineering. The Task Group thus found it necessary to repeat Richard Feynman's famous conclusion to his report on the first shuttle accident, the 1986 loss of the Challenger: "For a successful technology, reality must take precedence over public relations, for Nature cannot be fooled."[15]

By using PP to report technical work, presenters quickly damage their credibility—as was the case for NASA administrators and engineers pitching their usual PP decks to these 2 very serious review boards.

Both the Columbia Accident Investigation Board and the Return to Flight Task Group were filled with smart experienced people with spectacular credentials. These review boards examined what is probably the best evidence available on PP for technical work: hundreds of PP decks from a high-IQ government agency thoroughly practiced in PP. Both review boards concluded that (1) PowerPoint is an inappropriate tool for engineering reports, presentations, documentation and (2) the technical report is superior to PP. Matched up against alternative tools, PowerPoint lost.

Serious problems require a serious tool: written reports. For nearly all engineering and scientific communication, instead of PowerPoint, *the presentation and reporting software should be a word-processing program* capable of capturing, editing, and publishing text, tables, data graphics, images, and scientific notation. Replacing PowerPoint with Microsoft Word (or, better, a tool with non-proprietary universal formats) will make presentations and their audiences smarter. Of course full-screen projected images and videos are necessary; that is the one harmless use of PP. Meetings should center on concisely written reports on paper, not fragmented bulleted talking points projected up on the wall. A good model for the technical report is a scientific paper or commentary on a paper published in substantial scientific journals such as *Nature* or *Science*.

[13] *Final Report of the Return to Flight Task Group*, July 2005, 195.

[14] *Final Report of the Return to Flight Task Group*, July 2005, 195.

[15] Richard P. Feynman, *"What Do You Care What Other People Think? Further Adventures of a Curious Character* (New York, 1988), 237; and quoted by the *Final Report of the Return to Flight Task Group*, July 2005, 194.

## *High-Resolution Visual Channels Are Compromised by PowerPoint*

A TALK, which proceeds at a pace of 100 to 160 spoken words per minute, is not an especially high-resolution method of data transmission. Rates of transmitting *visual* evidence can be far higher. The artist Ad Reinhardt said, "As for a picture, if it isn't worth a thousand words, the hell with it." People can quickly look over tables with hundreds of numbers in the financial or sports pages in newspapers. People read 300 to 1,000 printed words a minute, and find their way around a printed map or a 35mm slide displaying 5 to 40 MB in the visual field. Often the visual channel is an intensely high-resolution channel.

Yet, in a strange reversal, nearly all PowerPoint slides that accompany talks have much *lower* rates of information transmission than the talk itself. Too often the images are content-free clip art, the statistical graphics don't show data, and the text is grossly impoverished. As shown in this table, *the PowerPoint slide typically shows 40 words, which is about 8 seconds of silent reading material.* The example slides in PP textbooks are particularly disturbing: in 28 books, which should use only first-rate examples, the median number of words per slide is 15, worthy of billboards, about 3 or 4 seconds of silent reading material.

This poverty of content has several sources. *The PP design style,* which uses only about 40% to 60% of the space available on a slide to show unique content, with all remaining space devoted to Phluff, bullets, frames, and branding. The *slide projection of text,* which requires very large type so the audience can see the words. Most importantly, *presenters who don't have all that much to say* (for example, among the 2,140 slides reported in this table, the really lightweight slides are found in the presentations made by educational administrators and their PR staff).

A vicious circle results. Thin content leads to boring presentations. To make them unboring, PP Phluff is added, damaging the content, making the presentation even more boring, requiring more Phluff . . . .

What to do? For serious presentations, it will be useful to replace PowerPoint slides with paper handouts showing words, numbers, data graphics, images together. High-resolution handouts allow viewers to contextualize, compare, narrate, and recast evidence. In contrast, data-thin, forgetful displays tend to make audiences ignorant and passive, and also to diminish the credibility of the presenter. Thin visual content prompts suspicions: "What are they leaving out? Is that all they know? Does the speaker think we're stupid?" "What are they hiding?" Sometimes PowerPoint's low resolution is said to promote a clarity of reading and thinking. Yet in visual reasoning, art, typography, cartography, even sculpture, *the quantity of detail is an issue completely separate from the difficulty of reading.*[16] Indeed, quite often, the more intense the detail, the *greater* the clarity and understanding—because meaning and reasoning are relentlessly *contextual.* Less is a bore.

| WORDS ON TEXT-ONLY POWERPOINT SLIDES | |
| --- | --- |
| 26 slides in the 3 Columbia reports by Boeing, median number of words per slide | 97 |
| 1,460 text-only slides in 189 PP reports posted on the internet and top-ranked by Google, March 2003, median number of words per slide | 40 |
| 654 slides in 28 PowerPoint textbooks, published 1997-2003, median number of words per slide | 15 |

[16] Edward Tufte, *Envisioning Information* (1990), 36-51.

## *The Hierarchical Bullet List Dilutes Thought*

LISTS often serve well for prompts, reminders, outlines, filing, and possibly for quick no-fooling-around messages. Lists have diverse architectures: elaborately ordered to disordered, linearly sequential to drifting around 2-space, and highly calibrated hierarchies of typographic dingbats to free-wheeling dingbat dingbats. In constructing lists, a certain convenience derives from their lack of syntactic and intellectual discipline, as each element consists of scattered words in fragmented pre-sentences.

PowerPoint promotes the hierarchical bullet list, surely the most widely used format in corporate and government presentations. Slides are filled with over-twiddly structures with some space left over for content. These formats usually require deeply indented lines for elements consisting of a few words, the power points. The more elaborate the hierarchy, the greater the loss of explanatory resolution, as the container dominates the thing contained.

It is unwise and arrogant to replace the sentence as the basic unit for explaining something. Especially as the byproduct of some marketing presentation software.

For the naive, bullet lists may create the appearance of hard-headed organized thought. But in the reality of day-to-day practice, the PP cognitive style is faux-analytical, with a bias towards promoting effects without causes. An analysis in the *Harvard Business Review* found generic, superficial, simplistic thinking in bullet lists widely used in business planning and corporate strategy:

> In every company we know, planning follows the standard format of the bullet outline. . . [But] bullet lists encourage us to be lazy . . .
>
> **Bullet lists are typically too generic.** They offer a series of things to do that could apply to any business. . . .
>
> **Bullets leave critical relationships unspecified.** Lists can communicate only three logical relationships: sequence (first to last in time); priority (least to most important or vice versa); or simple membership in a set (these items relate to one another in some way, but the nature of that relationship remains unstated). And a list can show only one of those relationships at a time.[17]

[17] Gordon Shaw, Robert Brown, Philip Bromiley, "Strategic Stories: How 3M is Rewriting Business Planning," *Harvard Business Review*, 76 (May-June, 1998), 44.

The bullet-list format collaborates thus with evasive presenters to promote *effects without causes*, as in the fragmented generic points of cheerleading strategic plans and the dreaded mission statement:

> ★ *Accelerate The Introduction Of New Products!!!*
> ★ *Accelerate Revenue Recognition!!!*

Better to say *who* will accelerate, and *what, how, when,* and *where* they will accelerate. An effective methodology for making such statements is the *sentence*, with subjects and predicates, nouns and verbs, agents and their effects. Identifying specific agents of action may also eventually assist forensic accountants and prosecutors in targeting those responsible for excessively accelerated recognition of revenue.

In presentations of plans, schemes, and strategies, bullet outlines get all confused even about simple, one-way causal models. Here, again from the *Harvard Business Review*, an analysis of bullets for business plans:

> Bullets leave critical assumptions about how the business works unstated. Consider these major objectives from a standard five-year strategic plan
>
> - Increase market share by 25%.
> - Increase profits by 30%.
> - Increase new-product introductions to ten a year.
>
> Implicit in this plan is a complex but unexplained vision of the organization, the market, and the customer. However, we cannot extrapolate that vision from the bullet list. The plan does not tell us how these objectives tie together and, in fact, many radically different strategies could be represented by these three simple points. Does improved marketing increase market share, which results in increased profits (perhaps from economies of scale), thus providing funds for increased new-product development?
>
> Market share $\longrightarrow$ Profits $\longrightarrow$ New-product development
>
> Or maybe new-product development will result in both increased profits and market share at once:
>
> New-product development $\longrightarrow$ Market share
> Profits
>
> Alternatively, perhaps windfall profits will let us just buy market share by stepping up advertising and new-product development:
>
> Profits $\longrightarrow$ New-product development $\longrightarrow$ Market share.[18]

It follows that more complex and realistic multivariate causal models are way over the head of the simplistic bullet-list format.

FOR scientists and engineers, a good way to help raise the quality of an analysis is to ask "What would Richard Feynman do?" The Feynman Principle helps with technical reporting. Feynman experienced the intense bullet outline style in his work on the first shuttle accident, the Challenger in 1986. He expressed his views clearly:

> Then we learned about "bullets"—little black circles in front of phrases that were supposed to summarize things. There was one after another of these little goddamn bullets in our briefing books and on slides.[19]

As analysis becomes more causal, multivariate, comparative, evidence-based, and resolution-intense, the more damaging the bullet list becomes. Scientists and engineers have communicated about complex matters for centuries without bullets. Richard Feynman wrote about much of physics—from classical mechanics to quantum electrodynamics—in three famous textbook volumes totalling 1800 pages. Those books use no bullets and only 2 levels of hierarchy, chapters and subheads within chapters. $\longrightarrow$

[18] Gordon Shaw, Robert Brown, Philip Bromiley, "Strategic Stories: How 3M is Rewriting Business Planning," *Harvard Business Review*, 76 (May-June, 1998), 44.

[19] Richard P. Feynman, *"What Do You Care What Other People Think?"* (New York, 1988), 126-127.

Page layout from Richard P. Feynman, Robert B. Leighton, and Matthew Sands, *The Feynman Lectures on Physics* (1963), vol. 1, 38.5:

*The Gettysburg PowerPoint Presentation*

The PP cognitive style is so distinctive and peculiar that presentations relying on standard ready-made templates sometimes appear as over-the-top parodies instead of the sad realities they are. Here is an intentional and ferocious parody: imagine Abraham Lincoln had used PowerPoint at Gettysburg. . . .

*Um, my name is Abraham Lincoln and, um, I must now reboot . . . .*

*As we see in the Organizational Overview slide, four score and seven years ago our fathers brought forth on this continent a new nation, conceived in liberty and dedicated to the proposition that all men are created equal. Now we are engaged in a great civil war, testing whether that nation or any nation so conceived and so dedicated can long endure. Next slide please. We are met on a great battlefield of that war. We have come to dedicate a portion of that field as a final resting place for those who here gave their lives that that nation might live. It is altogether fitting and proper that we should do this. But in a larger sense, we cannot dedicate, we cannot consecrate, we cannot hallow this ground. The brave men, living and dead who struggled here have consecrated it far above our poor power to add or detract. Next slide please. The world will little note nor long remember what we say here, but it can never forget what they did here. It is for us the living rather to be dedicated here to the unfinished work which they who fought here have thus far so*

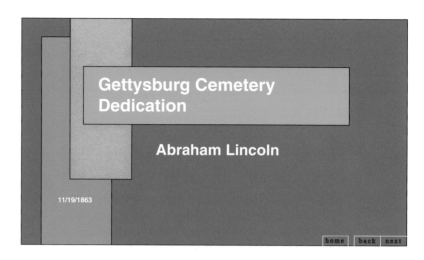

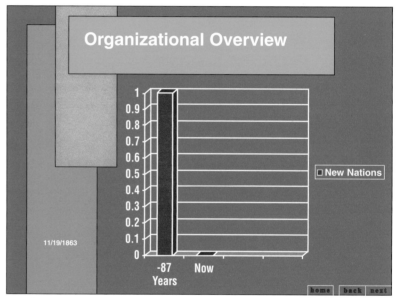

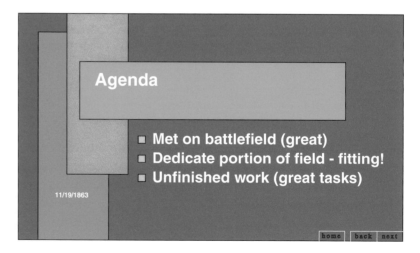

*nobly advanced. It is rather for us to be here dedicated to the great task remaining before us—that from these honored dead we take increased devotion to that cause for which they gave the last full measure of devotion, next slide please, that we here highly resolve that these dead shall not have died in vain, that this nation under God shall have a new birth of freedom, and that government of the people, by the people, for the people, shall not perish from the earth.*

This PowerPoint presentation was created by Peter Norvig; see www.norvig.com. The graph showing "-87 years" for Lincoln's "four score and seven years ago" is brilliant. Norvig notes that other slides were quickly constructed by means of the PP "AutoContent Wizard." In an essay in *The New Yorker* (May 28, 2001), Ian Parker describes the AutoContent Wizard as "a rare example of a product named in outright mockery of its target customers" (p. 76).

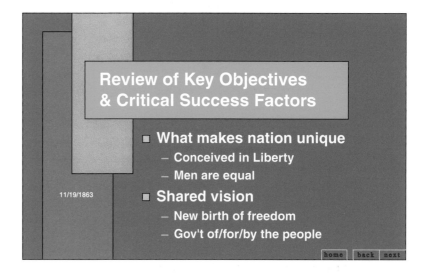

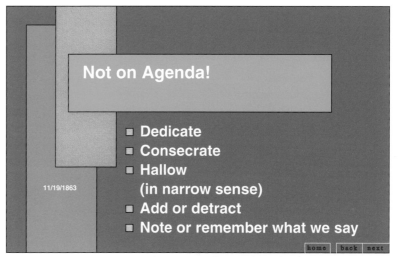

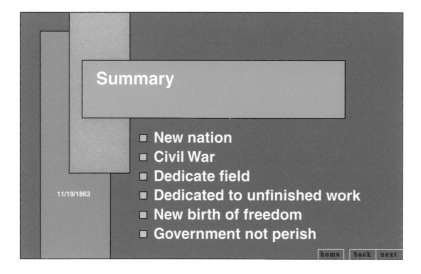

## PowerPoint and Statistical Evidence

To investigate the performance of PP for statistical data, let us consider an important and intriguing table of cancer survival rates relative to those without cancer for the same time period. Some 196 numbers and 57 words describe survival rates and their standard errors for 24 cancers:

### Estimates of relative survival rates, by cancer site[20]

| | % survival rates and their standard errors | | | | | | |
|---|---|---|---|---|---|---|---|
| | 5 year | | 10 year | | 15 year | | 20 year | |
| Prostate | 98.8 | 0.4 | 95.2 | 0.9 | 87.1 | 1.7 | 81.1 | 3.0 |
| Thyroid | 96.0 | 0.8 | 95.8 | 1.2 | 94.0 | 1.6 | 95.4 | 2.1 |
| Testis | 94.7 | 1.1 | 94.0 | 1.3 | 91.1 | 1.8 | 88.2 | 2.3 |
| Melanomas | 89.0 | 0.8 | 86.7 | 1.1 | 83.5 | 1.5 | 82.8 | 1.9 |
| Breast | 86.4 | 0.4 | 78.3 | 0.6 | 71.3 | 0.7 | 65.0 | 1.0 |
| Hodgkin's disease | 85.1 | 1.7 | 79.8 | 2.0 | 73.8 | 2.4 | 67.1 | 2.8 |
| Corpus uteri, uterus | 84.3 | 1.0 | 83.2 | 1.3 | 80.8 | 1.7 | 79.2 | 2.0 |
| Urinary, bladder | 82.1 | 1.0 | 76.2 | 1.4 | 70.3 | 1.9 | 67.9 | 2.4 |
| Cervix, uteri | 70.5 | 1.6 | 64.1 | 1.8 | 62.8 | 2.1 | 60.0 | 2.4 |
| Larynx | 68.8 | 2.1 | 56.7 | 2.5 | 45.8 | 2.8 | 37.8 | 3.1 |
| Rectum | 62.6 | 1.2 | 55.2 | 1.4 | 51.8 | 1.8 | 49.2 | 2.3 |
| Kidney, renal pelvis | 61.8 | 1.3 | 54.4 | 1.6 | 49.8 | 2.0 | 47.3 | 2.6 |
| Colon | 61.7 | 0.8 | 55.4 | 1.0 | 53.9 | 1.2 | 52.3 | 1.6 |
| Non-Hodgkin's | 57.8 | 1.0 | 46.3 | 1.2 | 38.3 | 1.4 | 34.3 | 1.7 |
| Oral cavity, pharynx | 56.7 | 1.3 | 44.2 | 1.4 | 37.5 | 1.6 | 33.0 | 1.8 |
| Ovary | 55.0 | 1.3 | 49.3 | 1.6 | 49.9 | 1.9 | 49.6 | 2.4 |
| Leukemia | 42.5 | 1.2 | 32.4 | 1.3 | 29.7 | 1.5 | 26.2 | 1.7 |
| Brain, nervous system | 32.0 | 1.4 | 29.2 | 1.5 | 27.6 | 1.6 | 26.1 | 1.9 |
| Multiple myeloma | 29.5 | 1.6 | 12.7 | 1.5 | 7.0 | 1.3 | 4.8 | 1.5 |
| Stomach | 23.8 | 1.3 | 19.4 | 1.4 | 19.0 | 1.7 | 14.9 | 1.9 |
| Lung and bronchus | 15.0 | 0.4 | 10.6 | 0.4 | 8.1 | 0.4 | 6.5 | 0.4 |
| Esophagus | 14.2 | 1.4 | 7.9 | 1.3 | 7.7 | 1.6 | 5.4 | 2.0 |
| Liver, bile duct | 7.5 | 1.1 | 5.8 | 1.2 | 6.3 | 1.5 | 7.6 | 2.0 |
| Pancreas | 4.0 | 0.5 | 3.0 | 1.5 | 2.7 | 0.6 | 2.7 | 0.8 |

Applying the PowerPoint templates for statistical graphics to this nice straightforward table yields the analytical disasters on the facing page. "Sweet songs never last too long on broken radios," wrote John Prine. These PP default-designs cause the data to explode into 6 separate chaotic slides, consuming 2.9 times the area of the table. *Everything* is wrong with these smarmy, incoherent graphs: uncomparative, thin data-density, chartjunk, encoded legends, meaningless color, logotype branding, indifference to content and evidence. Chartjunk is a clear sign of statistical stupidity; use these designs in your presentation, and your audience will quickly and correctly conclude that you don't know much about data and evidence.[21] Poking a finger into the eye of thought, these data graphics would turn into a nasty travesty if used for

[20] Redesigned table based on Hermann Brenner, "Long-term survival rates of cancer patients achieved by the end of the 20th century: a period analysis," *The Lancet*, 360 (October 12, 2002), 1131-1135. Brenner recalculates survival rates from data collected by the U.S. National Cancer Institute, 1973-1998, from the Surveillance, Epidemiology, and End Results Program.

[21] PP-style chartjunk occasionally shows up in graphics of evidence in scientific journals. Below, the clutter half-conceals thin data with some vibrating pyramids framed by an unintentional Necker illusion, as the 2 back planes optically flip to the front:

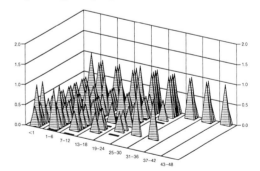

For such small data sets, usually a simple table will show the data more effectively than a graph, let alone a chartjunk graph. Source of graph: N. T. Kouchoukos, *et al.*, "Replacement of the Aortic Root with a Pulmonary Autograft in Children and Young Adults with Aortic-Valve Disease," *New England Journal of Medicine*, 330 (January 6, 1994), 4. On chartjunk, see Edward R. Tufte, *The Visual Display of Quantitative Information* (1983, 2001), chapter 5.

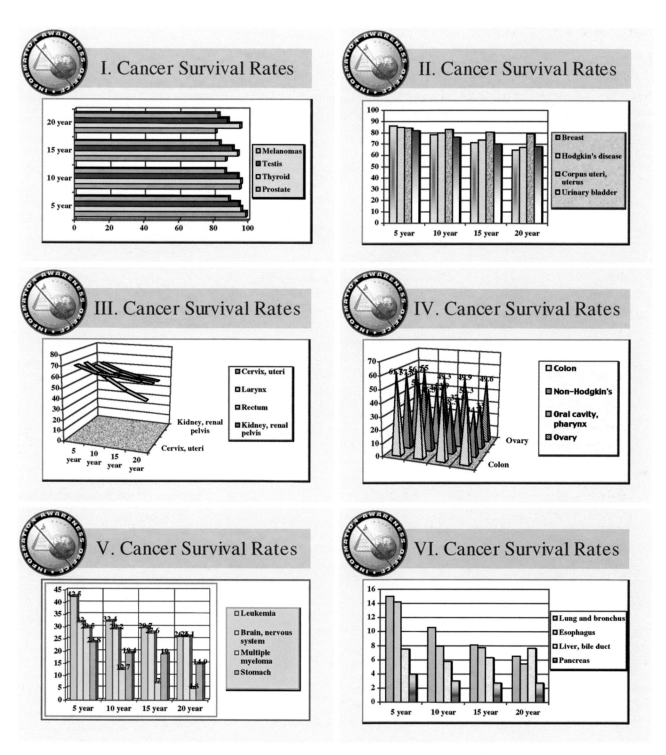

a serious purpose, such as cancer patients seeking to assess their survival chances. To deal with a product that messes up data with such systematic intensity must require an enormous insulation from statistical integrity and statistical reasoning by Microsoft PP executives and programmers, PP textbook writers, and presenters of such chartjunk.

The best way to show the cancer data is the original table with its good comparative structure and reporting of standard errors. And PP default graphics are not the way to see the data. Our table-graphic, however, does give something of a *visual idea* of time-gradients for survival for each cancer. Like the original table, every visual element in the graphic shows data. Slideware displays, in contrast, usually devote a majority of their space to things other than data.

Estimates of % survival rates

| | 5 year | 10 year | 15 year | 20 year |
|---|---|---|---|---|
| Prostate | 99 | 95 | 87 | 81 |
| Thyroid | 96 | 96 | 94 | 95 |
| Testis | 95 | 94 | 91 | 88 |
| Melanomas | 89 | 87 | 84 | 83 |
| Breast | 86 | 78 | 71 | 65 |
| Hodgkin's disease | 85 | 80 | 74 | 67 |
| Corpus uteri, uterus | 84 | 83 | 81 | 79 |
| Urinary, bladder | 82 | 76 | 70 | 68 |
| Cervix, uteri | 71 | 64 | 63 | 60 |
| Larynx | 69 | 57 | 46 | 38 |
| Rectum | 63 | 55 | 52 | 49 |
| Kidney, renal pelvis | 62 | 54 | 50 | 47 |
| Colon | 62 | 55 | 54 | 52 |
| Non-Hodgkin's | 58 | 46 | 38 | 34 |
| Oral cavity, pharynx | 57 | 44 | 38 | 33 |
| Ovary | 55 | 49 | 50 | 50 |
| Leukemia | 43 | 32 | 30 | 26 |
| Brain, nervous system | 32 | 29 | 28 | 26 |
| Multiple myeloma | 30 | 13 | 7 | 5 |
| Stomach | 24 | 19 | 19 | 15 |
| Lung and bronchus | 15 | 11 | 8 | 6 |
| Esophagus | 14 | 8 | 8 | 5 |
| Liver, bile duct | 8 | 6 | 6 | 8 |
| Pancreas | 4 | 3 | 3 | 3 |

## PowerPoint Stylesheets

THE PP cognitive style is propagated by the templates, textbooks, stylesheets, and complete pitches available for purchase. Some corporations and government agencies *require* employees to use designated PP Phluff and presentation logo-wear. With their strict generic formats, these designer stylesheets serve only to enforce the limitations of PowerPoint, compromising the presenter, the content, and, ultimately, the audience.

Here we see a witless PP pitch on how to make a witless PP pitch. Prepared at the Harvard School of Public Health by the "Instructional Computing Facility," these templates are uninformed by the practices of scientific publication and the rich intellectual history of evidence and analysis in public health. The templates do, however, emulate the format of reading primers for 6 year-olds.

Jane said, "Here is a ball.
See this blue ball, Sally.
Do you want this ball?"

Sally said, "I want my ball.
My ball is yellow.
It is a big, pretty ball."

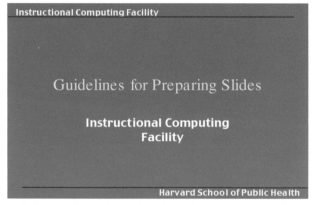

Stylesheet-makers often seek to leave *their* name on *your* show; "branding," as they say in the Marketing Department. In case you didn't notice, this presentation is from the "Instructional Computing Facility." But where are the names of the people responsible for this? No names appear on any of the 21 slides.

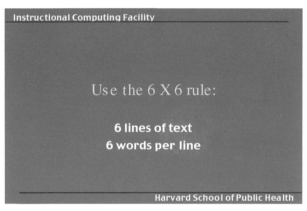

This must be the Haiku Rule for formatting scientific lectures. At least we're not limited to 17 syllables per slide. Above this slide, the rule can be seen in action—in a first-grade reading primer. The stylesheet typography, distinctly unscientific, uses a capital X instead of a multiplication sign.

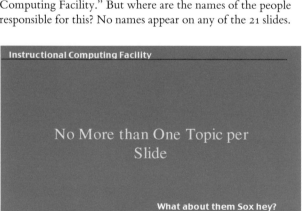

But this breaks up the evidence into arbitrary fragments. Why aren't we seeing examples from actual scientific reports? What are the Sox (a rather parochial reference) doing here? The inept PP typography persists: strange over-active indents, oddly chosen initial caps, typographic orphans on 3 of 4 slides.

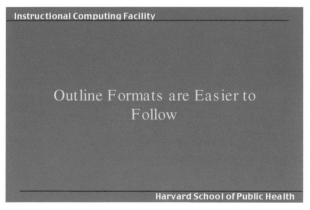

Why is this relevant to scientific presentations? Are there other principles than ease of following? Didn't the *Harvard Business Review* article indicate that bullet outlines corrupted thought? Text, imaging, and data for scientific presentations should be at the level of scientific journals, much *higher* resolution than speech.

Instructional Computing Facility

## Use Simple Tables to Present Numbers

| | Use Tables | For Your Numbers | But Not too Many |
|---|---|---|---|
| This row | 10 | 90 | 100 |
| This row | 0.6 | 0.4 | 1 |
| This row | 1 | 2 | 3 |
| That row | 1 | 2 | 3 |

Try not to make footnotes too small

**Harvard School of Public Health**

The stylesheet goes on to victimize statistical data, the fundamental evidence of public health. The table shows 12 numbers which is lousy for science, sports, weather, or financial data but standard for PowerPoint.[22] Table design is a complex and subtle matter in typographic work, but there is nothing thoughtful about design here. The unsourced numbers are not properly aligned, the row and column labels are awful, the units of measurement not given. This stylesheet of pseudoscience displays a flippant smirky attitude toward evidence. That attitude—*what counts are power and pitches, not truth and evidence*—also lurks within PowerPoint.

Consider now a real table. Bringing scientific methods to medical and demographic evidence, John Graunt's *Bills of Mortality* (1662) is the foundation work of public health. Graunt calculated the first tables of life expectancy, compared different causes of death, and even discussed defects in the evidence. His renowned "Table of Casualties" (at right) shows 1,855 different counts of death from 1629 to 1659. How fortunate that Graunt did not have PowerPoint and the assistance of the Harvard School of Public Health Instructional Computing Facility. Their silly guidelines above suggest the construction of 155 separate PowerPoint slides to show the data in Graunt's original table!

For tables, the analytical idea is to make comparisons. The number of possible pairwise comparisons in a table increases as the square of the number of cells.[23] In Graunt's table, 1,719,585 pairwise comparisons, of varying relevance to be sure, are within the eyespan of the inquiring mind. In contrast, the 155 tiny tables on 155 PP slides would offer only 10,230 pairwise comparisons, about 6 in 1,000 of those available in Graunt's original table. These PP tables would also block all sorts of interesting comparisons, such as time patterns over many years. What Graunt needs to do for his presentation at Harvard is simply to provide printed copies of his original table to everyone in the audience.

[22] Some 39 tables appear in our collection of 28 PP textbooks. These tables show an average (median) of 12 numbers each, which approaches the *Pravda* level. In contrast, sports and financial pages in newspapers routinely present tables with hundreds, even thousands of numbers. Below, we see a conventional weather table from a newspaper. The Harvard School of Public Health PP guidelines inform presenters that this data set will require 31 PP slides:

| **Africa** | Yesterday | Today | Tomorrow |
|---|---|---|---|
| Algiers | 82/ 66 0.55 | 85/ 60 S | 85/ 61 S |
| Cairo | 99/ 70 0 | 101/ 76 S | 96/ 76 S |
| Cape Town | 64/ 54 0.16 | 63/ 49 PC | 60/ 50 Sh |
| Dakar | 87/ 77 0.75 | 86/ 81 PC | 85/ 81 PC |
| Johannesburg | 69/ 42 0 | 73/ 42 S | 71/ 47 S |
| Nairobi | 75/ 55 0 | 78/ 56 PC | 78/ 56 PC |
| Tunis | 80/ 69 – | 87/ 73 PC | 85/ 71 PC |
| **Asia/Pacific** | Yesterday | Today | Tomorrow |
| Auckland | 59/ 45 0.12 | 58/ 44 Sh | 58/ 44 Sh |
| Bangkok | 91/ 82 0 | 91/ 79 Sh | 91/ 77 Sh |
| Beijing | 85/ 57 0 | 84/ 60 S | 78/ 65 PC |
| Bombay | 88/ 75 0.28 | 87/ 77 T | 88/ 78 T |
| Damascus | 96/ 55 0 | 98/ 59 S | 96/ 62 S |
| Hong Kong | 91/ 77 0 | 88/ 81 PC | 92/ 78 PC |
| Jakarta | 89/ 77 0 | 90/ 77 PC | 89/ 77 PC |
| Jerusalem | 87/ 64 0 | 88/ 66 S | 88/ 69 S |
| Karachi | 86/ 80 0 | 92/ 78 PC | 92/ 79 S |
| Manila | 86/ 75 – | 84/ 75 R | 87/ 78 R |
| New Delhi | 89/ 80 Tr | 88/ 76 Sh | 92/ 76 Sh |
| Riyadh | 98/ 69 0 | 102/ 74 S | 101/ 75 S |
| Seoul | 78/ 64 2.09 | 83/ 65 PC | 77/ 66 R |
| Shanghai | 75/ 69 0.06 | 86/ 76 Sh | 86/ 73 PC |
| Singapore | 87/ 78 Tr | 89/ 76 R | 89/ 78 Sh |
| Sydney | 68/ 53 0 | 71/ 51 PC | 71/ 48 PC |
| Taipei | 84/ 77 2.28 | 87/ 73 PC | 88/ 72 PC |
| Tehran | 93/ 73 0 | 87/ 73 S | 87/ 73 S |
| Tokyo | 89/ 77 0 | 91/ 79 Sh | 83/ 80 Sh |
| **Europe** | Yesterday | Today | Tomorrow |
| Amsterdam | 56/ 50 0.39 | 66/ 51 PC | 64/ 52 Sh |
| Athens | 87/ 75 0 | 90/ 75 S | 88/ 71 S |
| Berlin | 64/ 55 0.31 | 61/ 49 R | 68/ 52 PC |
| Brussels | 62/ 54 Tr | 66/ 53 PC | 65/ 52 Sh |
| Budapest | 72/ 59 0 | 75/ 55 S | 67/ 53 Sh |
| Copenhagen | 59/ 51 0.08 | 63/ 51 Sh | 63/ 52 PC |
| Dublin | 66/ 54 0.12 | 66/ 55 Sh | 63/ 47 PC |
| Edinburgh | 63/ 46 0.02 | 63/ 46 R | 64/ 48 PC |
| Frankfurt | 65/ 54 0.01 | 65/ 54 Sh | 66/ 50 PC |
| Geneva | 69/ 57 0.04 | 64/ 56 Sh | 65/ 50 PC |
| Helsinki | 63/ 45 0 | 62/ 46 PC | 63/ 45 PC |
| Istanbul | 84/ 60 0.01 | 79/ 69 Sh | 78/ 67 S |
| Kiev | 66/ 46 0 | 64/ 47 S | 64/ 46 S |
| Lisbon | 84/ 62 0 | 91/ 65 S | 90/ 67 S |
| London | 71/ 53 0.08 | 66/ 55 Sh | 69/ 55 PC |
| Madrid | 86/ 46 0 | 87/ 55 S | 87/ 57 S |
| Moscow | 55/ 41 0 | 64/ 40 S | 62/ 44 S |
| Nice | 78/ 62 0.01 | 78/ 65 S | 78/ 63 S |
| Oslo | 62/ 48 0 | 57/ 47 PC | 59/ 45 PC |
| Paris | 68/ 57 0 | 69/ 56 PC | 68/ 57 PC |
| Prague | 64/ 55 0.04 | 56/ 49 T | 63/ 49 Sh |
| Rome | 75/ 62 – | 79/ 61 S | 76/ 60 Sh |
| St. Petersburg | 59/ 39 0 | 66/ 46 S | 65/ 47 PC |
| Stockholm | 64/ 46 0 | 61/ 49 PC | 63/ 45 PC |
| Vienna | 64/ 59 0.16 | 65/ 53 PC | 66/ 52 Sh |
| Warsaw | 69/ 46 0 | 62/ 51 Sh | 65/ 49 PC |

[23] A table with n cells yields n(n - 1)/2 pairwise comparisons of cell entries.

John Graunt, *National and Political Observations mentioned in a following index, and made upon the Bills of Mortality. With reference to the Government, Religion, Trade, Growth, Ayre, Diseases, and the several Changes of the said City* (London, 1662); "The Table of Casualties" follows folio 74.

# THE TABLE OF CASUALTIES.

| The Years of our Lord | 1647 | 1648 | 1649 | 1650 | 1651 | 1652 | 1653 | 1654 | 1655 | 1656 | 1657 | 1658 | 1659 | 1660 | 1629 | 1630 | 1631 | 1632 | 1633 | 1634 | 1635 | 1636 | 1629 1630 1631 1632 | 1633 1634 1635 1636 | 1647 1648 1649 1650 | 1651 1652 1653 1654 | 1655 1656 1657 1658 | 1629 1649 1659 | In 20 Years. |
|---|---|---|---|---|---|---|---|---|---|---|---|---|---|---|---|---|---|---|---|---|---|---|---|---|---|---|---|---|---|
| Abortive, and ſtilborn | 335 | 329 | 327 | 351 | 389 | 381 | 384 | 433 | 483 | 419 | 463 | 467 | 421 | 544 | 499 | 439 | 410 | 445 | 500 | 475 | 507 | 523 | 1793 | 2005 | 1342 | 1587 | 1832 | 1247 | 8559 |
| Aged | 916 | 835 | 889 | 696 | 780 | 834 | 864 | 974 | 743 | 892 | 869 | 1176 | 909 | 1095 | 579 | 712 | 661 | 671 | 704 | 623 | 794 | 714 | 2475 | 2814 | 3336 | 3452 | 3680 | 2377 | 15757 |
| Ague, and Fever | 1260 | 884 | 751 | 970 | 1038 | 1212 | 1282 | 1371 | 689 | 875 | 999 | 1800 | 2303 | 2148 | 956 | 1091 | 1115 | 1108 | 953 | 1279 | 1622 | 2360 | 4418 | 6235 | 3865 | 4903 | 4363 | 4010 | 23784 |
| Apoplex, and ſodainly | 68 | 74 | 64 | 74 | 106 | 111 | 118 | 86 | 92 | 102 | 113 | 138 | 91 | 67 | 22 | 36 | | 17 | 24 | 35 | 26 | | 75 | 85 | 280 | 421 | 445 | 177 | 1306 |
| Bleach | | | 1 | 3 | 7 | 2 | | | | 1 | | | | | | | | | | | | | | | 4 | 9 | 1 | 1 | 15 |
| Blaſted | 4 | 1 | | | 6 | 6 | | | 4 | | 5 | 5 | 3 | 8 | 13 | 8 | 10 | 13 | 6 | 4 | | 4 | 54 | 14 | 5 | 12 | 14 | 16 | 99 |
| Bleeding | 3 | 2 | 5 | 1 | 3 | 4 | 3 | 2 | 7 | 3 | 5 | 4 | 7 | 2 | 5 | 2 | 5 | 4 | 4 | 3 | | | 16 | 7 | 11 | 12 | 19 | 17 | 65 |
| Bloudy Flux, Scouring, and Flux | 155 | 176 | 802 | 289 | 833 | 762 | 200 | 386 | 168 | 368 | 362 | 233 | 346 | 251 | 449 | 438 | 352 | 348 | 278 | 512 | 346 | 330 | 1587 | 1466 | 1422 | 2181 | 1161 | 1597 | 7818 |
| Burnt, and Scalded | 3 | 6 | 10 | 5 | 11 | 8 | 5 | 7 | 10 | 5 | 7 | 4 | 6 | 6 | 3 | 10 | 7 | 5 | 1 | 3 | 12 | 3 | 25 | 19 | 24 | 31 | 26 | 19 | 125 |
| Calenture | 1 | | | 1 | | 2 | 1 | 1 | | | 3 | | | | | | | | | | 1 | 3 | | 4 | 2 | 4 | 3 | | 13 |
| Cancer, Gangrene, and Fiſtula | 26 | 29 | 31 | 19 | 31 | 53 | 36 | 37 | 73 | 31 | 24 | 35 | 63 | 52 | 20 | 14 | 23 | 28 | 27 | 30 | 24 | 30 | 85 | 112 | 105 | 157 | 150 | 114 | 609 |
| Wolf | | | | 8 | | | | | | | | | | | | | | | | | | | | 8 | | | | | 8 |
| Canker, Sore-mouth, and Thruſh | 66 | 28 | 54 | 42 | 68 | 51 | 53 | 72 | 44 | 81 | 19 | 27 | 73 | 68 | 6 | 4 | 4 | 1 | | | 5 | 74 | 15 | 79 | 190 | 244 | 161 | 133 | 689 |
| Childbed | 161 | 106 | 114 | 117 | 206 | 213 | 158 | 192 | 177 | 201 | 236 | 225 | 226 | 194 | 150 | 157 | 112 | 171 | 132 | 143 | 163 | 230 | 590 | 668 | 498 | 769 | 839 | 490 | 3364 |
| Chriſomes, and Infants | 1369 | 1254 | 1065 | 990 | 1237 | 1280 | 1050 | 1343 | 1089 | 1393 | 1162 | 1144 | 858 | 1123 | 2596 | 2378 | 2035 | 2268 | 2130 | 2315 | 2113 | 1895 | 9277 | 8453 | 4678 | 4910 | 4788 | 4519 | 32106 |
| Colick, and Wind | 103 | 71 | 85 | 82 | 76 | 102 | 80 | 101 | 85 | 120 | 113 | 179 | 116 | 167 | 48 | 57 | | | | | 37 | 50 | 105 | 87 | 341 | 359 | 497 | 247 | 1389 |
| Cold, and Cough | | | | | | | 41 | 36 | 21 | 58 | 30 | 31 | 33 | 24 | 10 | 58 | 51 | 55 | 45 | 54 | 50 | 57 | 174 | 207 | 00 | 77 | 140 | 43 | 598 |
| Conſumption, and Cough | 2423 | 2200 | 2388 | 1988 | 2350 | 2410 | 2286 | 2868 | 2606 | 3184 | 2757 | 3610 | 2982 | 3414 | 1827 | 1910 | 1713 | 1797 | 1754 | 1955 | 2080 | 2477 | 5157 | 8266 | 8999 | 9914 | 12157 | 7197 | 44487 |
| Convulſion | 684 | 491 | 530 | 493 | 569 | 653 | 606 | 828 | 702 | 1027 | 807 | 841 | 742 | 1031 | 52 | 87 | 18 | 241 | 221 | 386 | 418 | 709 | 498 | 1734 | 2198 | 2656 | 3377 | 1324 | 9073 |
| Cramp | | | 1 | | | | | | | | | | | | | | 1 | 0 | 0 | 0 | 0 | 0 | 01 | 00 | 01 | 0 | 0 | 1 | 2 |
| Cut of the Stone | | 2 | 1 | 3 | | 1 | 1 | 2 | 4 | 1 | 3 | 5 | 46 | 48 | | | | 5 | 1 | 5 | 2 | 2 | 5 | 10 | 6 | 4 | 13 | 47 | 38 |
| Dropſy, and Tympany | 185 | 434 | 421 | 508 | 444 | 556 | 617 | 704 | 660 | 706 | 631 | 931 | 646 | 872 | 235 | 252 | 279 | 280 | 266 | 250 | 329 | 389 | 048 | 1734 | 1538 | 2321 | 2982 | 1302 | 9623 |
| Drowned | 47 | 40 | 30 | 27 | 49 | 50 | 53 | 30 | 43 | 45 | 63 | 60 | 57 | 48 | 43 | 33 | 29 | 34 | 37 | 32 | 32 | 45 | 139 | 147 | 144 | 182 | 215 | 130 | 827 |
| Exceſſive drinking | | | 2 | | | | | | | | | | | | | | | | | | | | | | 2 | | | 2 | 2 |
| Executed | 8 | 17 | 29 | 43 | 24 | 12 | 19 | 21 | 19 | 22 | 20 | 18 | 7 | 18 | 19 | 13 | 12 | 18 | 13 | 13 | 13 | 13 | 62 | 52 | 97 | 76 | 79 | 55 | 384 |
| Fainted in a Bath | | | | | 1 | | | | | | | | | | | | | | | | | | | | | 1 | | | 1 |
| Falling-Sickneſs | 3 | 2 | 2 | 3 | | 3 | 4 | 1 | 4 | 3 | 1 | | 4 | 5 | 3 | 10 | 7 | 7 | 2 | 5 | 6 | 8 | 27 | 21 | 10 | 8 | 8 | 9 | 74 |
| Flox, and ſmall pox | 139 | 400 | 1190 | 184 | 525 | 1279 | 139 | 812 | 1294 | 823 | 835 | 409 | 1523 | 354 | 72 | 40 | 58 | 531 | 72 | 1354 | 293 | 127 | 701 | 1846 | 1913 | 2755 | 3361 | 2785 | 10576 |
| Found dead in the Streets | 6 | 6 | 9 | 8 | 7 | 9 | 14 | 4 | 3 | 4 | 9 | 11 | 2 | 6 | 18 | 33 | 26 | 6 | 13 | 8 | 24 | 24 | 83 | 69 | 29 | 34 | 27 | 29 | 243 |
| French-Pox | 18 | 29 | 15 | 18 | 21 | 20 | 20 | 20 | 29 | 23 | 25 | 53 | 51 | 31 | 17 | 12 | 12 | 12 | 7 | 17 | 12 | 22 | 53 | 48 | 80 | 81 | 130 | 83 | 392 |
| Frighted | 4 | 4 | 1 | | 3 | | 2 | | 1 | 1 | | | | 9 | 1 | | | 1 | | | | 3 | 2 | 3 | 9 | 5 | 2 | 2 | 21 |
| Gout | 9 | 5 | 12 | 9 | 7 | 7 | 5 | 6 | 8 | 7 | 8 | 13 | 14 | 2 | 2 | 5 | 3 | 4 | 4 | 5 | 7 | 8 | 14 | 24 | 35 | 25 | 36 | 28 | 134 |
| Grief | 12 | 13 | 16 | 7 | 17 | 14 | 11 | 17 | 10 | 13 | 10 | 12 | 13 | 4 | 18 | 20 | 22 | 11 | 14 | 17 | 5 | 20 | 71 | 56 | 48 | 59 | 45 | 47 | 279 |
| Hanged, and made-away themſelves | 11 | 10 | 13 | 14 | 9 | 14 | 15 | 9 | 14 | 16 | 24 | 18 | 11 | 36 | 8 | 8 | 6 | 15 | | 3 | 8 | 7 | 37 | 18 | 48 | 47 | 72 | 32 | 222 |
| Head-Ach | | 1 | 11 | 2 | | 2 | 6 | 6 | 5 | 3 | 4 | 5 | 35 | 26 | | | | | | | 4 | 2 | 0 | 6 | 14 | 14 | 17 | 46 | 051 |
| Jaundice | 57 | 35 | 39 | 49 | 41 | 43 | 57 | 71 | 61 | 41 | 46 | 77 | 102 | 76 | 47 | 59 | 35 | 43 | 35 | 45 | 54 | 63 | 184 | 197 | 180 | 212 | 225 | 188 | 998 |
| Jaw-faln | 1 | 1 | | | 3 | | | 2 | 2 | | 3 | 1 | | | 10 | 16 | 13 | 8 | 10 | 10 | 4 | 11 | 47 | 35 | 02 | 5 | 6 | 10 | 95 |
| Impoſtume | 75 | 61 | 65 | 59 | 80 | 105 | 79 | 90 | 92 | 122 | 80 | 134 | 105 | 96 | 58 | 76 | 73 | 74 | 50 | 62 | 73 | 130 | 282 | 315 | 260 | 354 | 428 | 228 | 1639 |
| Itch | | 1 | | | | | | | | | | | | | | | | | 10 | | | | 00 | 10 | 01 | | | | 11 |
| Killed by ſeveral Accidents | 27 | 57 | 39 | 94 | 47 | 45 | 57 | 58 | 52 | 43 | 52 | 47 | 55 | 47 | 54 | 55 | 47 | 46 | 49 | 41 | 51 | 60 | 202 | 201 | 217 | 207 | 194 | 148 | 1021 |
| King's Evil | 27 | 26 | 22 | 19 | 22 | 20 | 26 | 26 | 27 | 24 | 23 | 28 | 28 | 54 | 16 | 25 | 18 | 38 | 35 | 20 | 26 | 69 | 97 | 150 | 94 | 94 | 102 | 66 | 537 |
| Lethargy | 3 | 4 | 2 | 4 | 4 | 4 | 3 | 10 | 9 | 4 | 6 | 2 | 6 | 4 | 1 | | 2 | 2 | 3 | | 2 | 2 | 5 | 7 | 13 | 21 | 21 | 9 | 67 |
| Leproſy | | | 1 | | | | | | | | | 1 | | 2 | 2 | | | | | | 2 | | 2 | 2 | 1 | | 1 | 3 | 06 |
| Livergrown, Spleen, and Rickets | 53 | 46 | 56 | 59 | 65 | 72 | 67 | 65 | 52 | 50 | 38 | 51 | 8 | 15 | 94 | 112 | 99 | 87 | 82 | 77 | 98 | 99 | 392 | 356 | 213 | 269 | 191 | 158 | 1421 |
| Lunatique | 12 | 18 | 6 | 11 | 7 | 11 | 9 | 12 | 6 | 7 | 13 | 5 | 14 | 14 | 6 | 11 | 6 | 5 | 4 | 2 | 2 | 5 | 28 | 13 | 47 | 39 | 31 | 26 | 158 |
| Meagrom | 12 | 13 | | 5 | 8 | 6 | 6 | 14 | 3 | 6 | 7 | 6 | 5 | 4 | | | 24 | | | | | 22 | 24 | 22 | 30 | 34 | 22 | 05 | 132 |
| Meaſles | 5 | 92 | 3 | 33 | 33 | 62 | 8 | 52 | 11 | 153 | 15 | 80 | 6 | 74 | 42 | 2 | 3 | 80 | 21 | 33 | 27 | 12 | 127 | 83 | 133 | 155 | 259 | 51 | 757 |
| Mother | 2 | | | | | 1 | 1 | 2 | 2 | 3 | | 3 | 1 | 8 | 1 | | | | | | | 3 | 01 | 3 | 2 | 4 | 8 | 02 | 18 |
| Murdered | 3 | 2 | 7 | 5 | 4 | 3 | 3 | 3 | 9 | 6 | 5 | 7 | 70 | 20 | | | 3 | 7 | | 6 | 5 | 8 | 10 | 19 | 17 | 13 | 27 | 77 | 86 |
| Overlayd, and ſtarved at Nurſe | 25 | 22 | 36 | 28 | 28 | 29 | 30 | 36 | 58 | 53 | 44 | 50 | 46 | 43 | 4 | 10 | 13 | 7 | 8 | 14 | 10 | 14 | 34 | 46 | 111 | 123 | 215 | 86 | 529 |
| Palſy | 27 | 21 | 19 | 20 | 23 | 20 | 29 | 18 | 22 | 23 | 20 | 22 | 17 | 21 | 17 | 23 | 17 | 25 | 14 | 21 | 25 | 17 | 82 | 77 | 87 | 90 | 87 | 53 | 423 |
| Plague | 3597 | 611 | 67 | 15 | 23 | 16 | 6 | 16 | 9 | 6 | 4 | 14 | 36 | 14 | | 1317 | 274 | 8 | | 1 | | 10400 | 1599 | 10401 | 4290 | 61 | 33 | 103 | 16384 |
| Plague in the Guts | | | | 1 | | 110 | 32 | | 37 | 315 | 446 | | 253 | 402 | | | | | | | | | 00 | 00 | 61 | 142 | 844 | 253 | 991 |
| Pleuriſy | 30 | 26 | 13 | 20 | 23 | 19 | 17 | 23 | 10 | 9 | 17 | 16 | 12 | 10 | 26 | 24 | 26 | 36 | 21 | | 45 | 24 | 112 | 90 | 89 | 72 | 52 | 51 | 415 |
| Poyſoned | | 3 | | 7 | | | | | | | | | | | | | | | 2 | | | 2 | 00 | 4 | 10 | 00 | 00 | 00 | 14 |
| Purples, and ſpotted Fever | 145 | 47 | 43 | 65 | 54 | 60 | 75 | 89 | 56 | 52 | 56 | 126 | 368 | 146 | 32 | 58 | 58 | 38 | 24 | 125 | 245 | 397 | 186 | 791 | 300 | 278 | 290 | 243 | 1845 |
| Quinſy, and Sore-throat | 14 | 11 | 12 | 17 | 24 | 20 | 18 | 9 | 15 | 13 | 7 | 10 | 21 | 14 | 01 | 8 | 6 | 7 | 24 | 04 | 5 | 22 | 22 | 55 | 54 | 71 | 45 | 34 | 247 |
| Rickets | 150 | 224 | 216 | 190 | 260 | 329 | 229 | 372 | 347 | 458 | 317 | 476 | 441 | 521 | | | | | | 14 | 49 | 50 | 00 | 113 | 780 | 1190 | 1598 | 657 | 3681 |
| Mother, riſing of the Lights | 150 | 92 | 115 | 120 | 134 | 138 | 135 | 178 | 166 | 212 | 203 | 228 | 210 | 249 | 44 | 72 | 99 | 98 | 60 | 84 | 72 | 104 | 309 | 220 | 777 | 585 | 809 | 369 | 2700 |
| Rupture | 16 | 7 | 7 | 6 | 7 | 16 | 7 | 15 | 11 | 20 | 19 | 18 | 12 | 28 | 2 | 6 | 4 | 9 | 4 | 3 | 10 | 13 | 21 | 30 | 36 | 45 | 68 | 2 | 201 |
| Scal'd-head | 2 | | | | 1 | | | | 2 | | | | | | | | | | | | | | | | 2 | 1 | 2 | | 05 |
| Scurvy | 32 | 20 | 21 | 21 | 29 | 43 | 41 | 44 | 103 | 71 | 82 | 82 | 95 | 12 | 5 | 7 | 9 | | 9 | | 00 | 25 | 33 | 34 | 94 | 132 | 300 | 115 | 593 |
| Smothered, and ſtifled | | | 2 | | | | | | | | | | | | | 24 | | | | | | | 24 | | 2 | | | 2 | 26 |
| Sores, Ulcers, broken and bruiſed | 15 | 17 | 17 | 16 | 26 | 32 | 25 | 32 | 23 | 34 | 40 | 47 | 61 | 48 | 23 | | 20 | 48 | 19 | 19 | 22 | 29 | 91 | 89 | 65 | 115 | 144 | 141 | 504 |
| Shot (Limbs | | | | | | | | | | | | | 7 | 20 | | | | | | | | | | | | | | 07 | 27 |
| Spleen | 12 | 17 | | | | | 13 | 13 | | 6 | 2 | 5 | 7 | 7 | | | | | | | | | | | 29 | 26 | 13 | 07 | 68 |
| Shingles | | | | | | | | | | | | | 1 | | | | | | 1 | | | | | 1 | | | | 1 | 2 |
| Starved | | 4 | 8 | 7 | 1 | 2 | 1 | 1 | 3 | 1 | 3 | 6 | 7 | 14 | | | | | | | | | 14 | | 19 | 5 | 13 | 29 | 51 |
| Stitch | | | | 1 | | | | | | | | | | | | | | | | | | | | | 1 | | | | 1 |
| Stone, and Strangury | 45 | 42 | 29 | 28 | 50 | 41 | 44 | 38 | 49 | 57 | 72 | 69 | 22 | 30 | | | 58 | 56 | 58 | 49 | 33 | 45 | 114 | 185 | 144 | 173 | 247 | 51 | 863 |
| Sciatica | | | | | | | | | | | | | | 2 | | | | 1 | 3 | | 1 | 6 | 1 | 4 | | | | | 15 |
| Stopping of the Stomach | 29 | 29 | 30 | 33 | 55 | 67 | 66 | 107 | 94 | 145 | 129 | 277 | 186 | 214 | | | | | | | | 6 | | 6 | 121 | 295 | 247 | 216 | 669 |
| Surfet | 217 | 137 | 136 | 123 | 104 | 177 | 178 | 212 | 128 | 161 | 137 | 218 | 202 | 192 | 63 | 157 | 149 | 86 | 104 | 114 | 132 | 371 | 445 | 721 | 613 | 671 | 644 | 401 | 3094 |
| Swine-Pox | 4 | 4 | 3 | | | | 1 | 4 | 2 | 1 | 1 | 1 | | | 5 | 8 | 4 | 6 | 3 | | 10 | | 23 | 13 | 11 | 5 | 5 | 10 | 57 |
| Teeth, and Worms | 767 | 597 | 540 | 598 | 709 | 905 | 691 | 1131 | 803 | 1198 | 878 | 1036 | 839 | 1008 | 440 | 506 | 335 | 470 | 432 | 454 | 539 | 1207 | 1751 | 2632 | 2502 | 3436 | 3915 | 1819 | 14236 |
| Tiffick | 62 | 47 | | | | | | | | | | | | | 8 | 12 | 14 | 34 | 23 | 15 | 27 | | 68 | 65 | 109 | | | 8 | 242 |
| Thruſh | | | | | | | | | | | 57 | 66 | | | 15 | 23 | 17 | 40 | 28 | 31 | 34 | | 95 | 93 | | | 123 | 15 | 211 |
| Vomiting | 1 | 6 | 3 | 7 | 4 | 6 | 3 | 14 | 7 | 27 | 16 | 19 | 8 | 10 | 1 | 4 | 1 | 1 | 2 | 5 | 6 | 3 | 7 | 16 | 17 | 27 | 69 | 12 | 136 |
| Worms | 147 | 107 | 105 | 65 | 85 | 86 | 53 | | | | | | | | 19 | 31 | 28 | 27 | 19 | 28 | 27 | | 105 | 74 | 424 | 224 | | 124 | 830 |
| Wen | 1 | | 1 | | 2 | 2 | | | 1 | | 1 | 2 | 1 | 1 | | | 1 | | 4 | | | | 1 | 4 | 2 | 4 | 4 | 2 | 15 |
| Sodainly | | | | | | | | | | | | | | | 63 | 59 | 37 | 62 | 58 | 62 | 78 | 34 | 221 | 233 | | | | 63 | 454 |

## PP Slide Formats for Paper Reports and Computer Screens Are Ridiculous and Lazy

In addition accompanying a talk, PP slides are printed out on paper, attached to emails, posted on the internet. Unfortunately, PP slides on paper and computer screen *replicate and intensify* all the problems of the PP cognitive style. Such slides extend the reach of PP's proprietary closed-document format since PP capabilities are necessary to see the slides. This short-run convenience to presenters and long-run benefit to Microsoft come at an enormous cost to the content and the audience.

As those who have disconsolately flipped through pages and pages of printed-out PP slide decks already know, such reports are physically thick and intellectually thin. Recall that the NASA Return to Flight Task Group observed a massive thinness in the PP closure reports. The resolution of printed-out slide decks is remarkably low, approaching dementia. This data table compares the information in one image-equivalent for books (one page), for the internet (one screen), and for PP (one slide). A single page in the *Physicians' Desk Reference* shows 54 typical PP slide-equivalents of information, and the whole very thick book equals a deck of 181,000 slides. A single page of an Elmore Leonard novel equals 13 typical PP slides. Nonfiction best-sellers show information at densities 10 to 50 times those of printed-out PP decks.

People see, read, and think all the time at intensities vastly greater than those presented in printed PP slides. Instead of showing a long sequence of tiny information-fragments on slides, and instead of dumping those slides onto paper, report makers should have the courtesy to write a real report (which might also be handed out at a meeting) and address their readers as serious people. PP templates are a lazy and ridiculous way to format printed reports.

PP slides also format information on computer screens. Presenters post their slides; then readers, if any, march through one slide after another on the computer screen. Popular news sites on the internet show 10 to 15 times more information on a computer screen than a typical PP slide on a computer screen. The shuttle Columbia reports prepared by Boeing, sent by email in PP format to be viewed on computer screens, were running at information densities of 20% of major news sites on the internet, as the table shows.

*The PP slide format has the worst signal/noise ratio of any known method of communication on paper or computer screen.* Extending PowerPoint to embrace paper and internet screens pollutes those display methods.

### CHARACTER COUNTS AND DENSITY PER PAGE-IMAGE

| | CHARACTERS PER PAGE | DENSITY: CHARACTERS/IN$^2$ |
|---|---|---|
| **BEST SELLING BOOKS** | | |
| *Physicians' Desk Reference* | 13,600 | 168 |
| *Your Income Tax* | 10,400 | 118 |
| *World Almanac* | 9,800 | 232 |
| *Joy of Cooking* | 5,700 | 108 |
| *The Merck Manual* | 4,700 | 117 |
| *Guinness Book of World Records* | 4,600 | 162 |
| *Consumer Reports Buying Guide* | 3,900 | 112 |
| *How to Cook Everything* | 3,900 | 53 |
| *Maximum Bob* (Elmore Leonard) | 3,100 | 115 |
| *Baby and Child Care* | 2,500 | 95 |
| | | |
| **NEWS SITES ON THE INTERNET** | | |
| Google News | 4,100 | 44 |
| New York Times | 4,100 | 43 |
| People's Daily (China) | 4,100 | 43 |
| Pravda | 4,100 | 43 |
| Los Angeles Times | 4,000 | 42 |
| BBC News | 3,400 | 36 |
| CNN | 3,300 | 35 |
| Yahoo | 3,200 | 34 |
| Time | 2,700 | 28 |
| MSNBC | 2,400 | 26 |
| | | |
| **POWERPOINT SLIDE FORMAT USED ON PAPER OR COMPUTER SCREEN** | | |
| Columbia reports by Boeing | 630 | 7 |
| 1,460 text slides in 189 PP reports | 250 | 3 |
| 654 text slides in 28 PP textbooks | 98 | 1 |
| Content-free slides | 0 | 0 |

## Competitive Analysis of Presentation Tools

OUR comparisons of various presentation tools in action indicate that PowerPoint is intellectually outperformed by competing tools. For the 10 case studies and 32 control samples, PP flunks the comparative tests, except for beating out *Pravda* in the statistical graphics competition.

Some of these comparisons are for *the same users with the same content.* Matched comparisons control for selection effects, such as the entertaining hypothesis that PP is a stupidity magnet, differentially attracting inept presenters with lightweight content (and thereby making PP look bad). Our evidence helps isolate PP effects, independent of user or content. Such comparisons—*Consumer Reports* style—provide a competitive analysis of presentation tools. In these tests, PP's poor performance cannot be blamed on its users. For example, in the shuttle investigations, given that the presenters are NASA engineers and the content is rocket science, which then is the better presentation method, PP or technical reports?

The scope of our evidence is limited. Nearly all the evidence is drawn from *serious presentations,* with explanations to understand, evidence to evaluate, problems to solve, decisions to make, and, in several examples, lives to save. It is hard to know how many presentations are serious. Perhaps 25% to 75%, depending very much upon the substantive field.

## What Are the Causes of Visual Presentations?

AN important but complex issue in evaluating visual presentations, including PowerPoint, is *what are the causes of a presentation?* What are the contributions of content quality, presenter skills, presentation methods, cognitive styles, and prevailing standards of integrity? To begin with, reasonably certain answers are that the causal structure is multivariate, that causes tend to interact and are not independent of one another, and that improvements will result from working on all factors.

George Orwell's classic essay "Politics and the English Language" gets right the interplay between quality of thought and cognitive style of presentation: "The English language becomes ugly and inaccurate because our thoughts are foolish, but the slovenliness of our language makes it easier for us to have foolish thoughts." Imagine Orwell writing about PP: "PowerPoint becomes ugly and inaccurate because our thoughts are foolish, but the slovenliness of PowerPoint makes it easier for us to have foolish thoughts." The PP cognitive style is familiar to readers of Orwell's remarkable and prescient novel *1984.*

WAR IS PEACE

WAR IS PEACE

FREEDOM IS SLAVERY

WAR IS PEACE

FREEDOM IS SLAVERY

IGNORANCE IS STRENGTH

Or consider the NASA presentations. What are the causes of the dreaded Engineering by PowerPoint? Engineers incapable of communicating by means of standard technical reports? Lack of intellectual rigor? Designer guidelines and bureaucratic norms that insist on PP for all presentations, regardless of content? The cognitive style of PowerPoint? A bureaucracy infected throughout by the pitch culture? The PowerPoint monopoly and the consequent lack of innovative and high-quality software for technical communication? A Conway's Law interaction of causes? Some or all of these factors? In what proportion?

Sorting all this out is not possible. Nonetheless, under most reasonable allocations of causal responsibility, the practical advice remains the same: To make smarter presentations, try smarter tools. Technical reports are smarter than PowerPoint. Sentences are smarter than the grunts of bullet points. PP templates for statistical graphics and data tables are hopeless.

ART historians reason about the causes of visual presentations. What can we learn from their work? To explain artistic productions, art historians make use of 4 grand explanatory variables: (1) differences in styles in art, (2) differences in artists working within a given style, (3) interplay among styles and artists, and (4) sources of new styles.

The prevailing *style* of a given period and place profoundly affects the character of visual presentations. Art history textbooks are written as narratives of distinctive, clearly identifiable styles: Prehistoric, Egyptian, Near Eastern, Classical, Byzantine, Islamic, Baroque, Renaissance, Far Eastern, Romanticism, African, Impressionism, Cubism. In the long history of representative art, the physical objects represented in art did not change all that much, nor did the artists' retinal images of those objects. Big changes in art resulted from changes in style. Style matters.

Those caught up *within a single style* of visual production, however, must necessarily explain differences in quality by reference to the skills and character of particular presenters, for style is a given. This is the method of the standard defense of PowerPoint, a defense that mobilizes the second grand explanatory variable, presenter variability, as the major determinant of visual productions. Lousy presentations are said to be *the fault of inept PP users, not the fault of PP.* Blame the user, not the cognitive style of the presentation tool, not the PP pitch culture.

That is sometimes the case, but causal responsibility for presentations is more complicated than that. Other explanatory variables of visual productions—cognitive style and quality of presentation tools, user and style interactions, context, character of the content—must be taken into account. Thus Orwell's Principle, for example, sensibly avoids mono-causal explanations: "The English language becomes ugly and inaccurate because our thoughts are foolish, but the slovenliness of our language makes it easier for us to have foolish thoughts." And thus our comparisons of the PP cognitive style with other tools; thus our analysis of the PP metaphors of marketing and hierarchy at work and play in bureaucracies.

What about some modest incremental reforms in the cognitive style of PowerPoint? The record is not promising. Throughout many versions of PP, the intellectual level and analytical quality has rarely improved. New releases feature ever more elaborated PP Phluff and therapeutic measures for troubled presenters. These self-parodying elaborations have made each new release *different* from the previous—but not smarter. PP competes only with itself: there are no incentives for meaningful change in a monopoly product with an 86% gross profit margin (as reported in antitrust proceedings). In a competitive market, producers must improve products and must operate under a philosophy that the customer is always right. Only monopolies can blame consumers for poor performances.

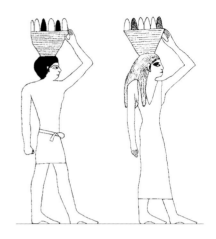

A better cognitive style for presentations is needed, a style that respects, encourages, and cooperates with evidence and thought. PowerPoint is like being trapped in the style of early Egyptian flatland cartoons rather than using the more effective tools of Renaissance visual representation.

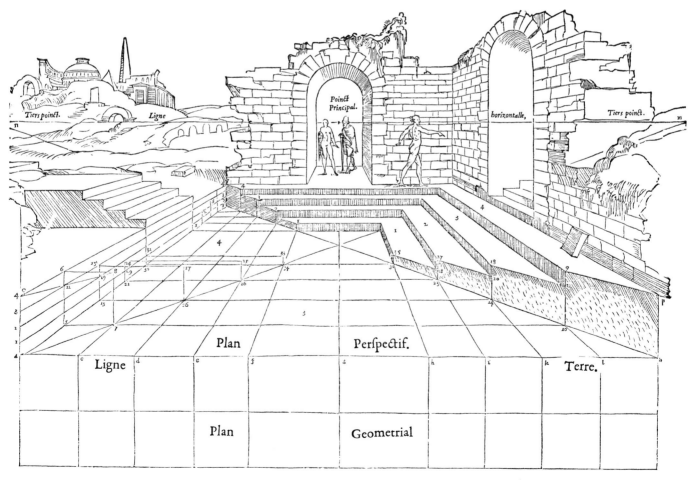

Jean Cousin, *Livre de perspective* (Paris, 1560), I iij.

## Improving Presentations

AT a minimum, we should choose presentation tools that *do no harm* to content. Yet PowerPoint promotes a cognitive style that disrupts and trivializes evidence. PP presentations too often resemble a school play: very loud, very slow, and very simple. Since $10^{10}$ to $10^{11}$ PP slides are produced yearly, that is a lot of harm to communication with colleagues.

PowerPoint is a competent slide manager, but a Projector Operating System should not impose Microsoft's cognitive style on our presentations. PP has some occasionally competent low-end design tools and way too many Phluff tools. PP might help show a few talking points at informal meetings, but instead why not simply print out an agenda for everyone?

For making serious presentations, replace PP with word-processing or page-layout software. To make this transition in large organizations requires a straightforward executive order: *From now on your presentation software is Microsoft Word not PowerPoint. Get used to it.*

Someday there will be a serious technical reporting tool better than a word-processor. This tool would combine a variety of page-layout templates (scientific formats uninfected by marketing communications outreach specialists); publication-quality tools for reporting statistical evidence in graphs and tables (designed by statisticians not commercial artists); mathematical notation (allowing NASA engineers to use exponents); a scientific spellchecker and thesaurus; open-document non-proprietary formats; large-paper color printing of reports; and within-document editing of words and graphics. This tool design should be driven by the necessities of *evidence display*, not pitching.

At a talk, paper handouts of a technical report effectively show text, data graphics, images. Printed materials bring information transfer rates in presentations up to that of everyday material in newspaper sports and financial pages, books, and internet news sites. An excellent paper size for presentation handouts is A3, 30 by 42 cm or about 11 by 17 inches, folded in half to make 4 pages. That one piece of paper, the 4-pager, can show images with 1,200 dpi resolution, up to 60,000 characters of words and numbers, detailed tables worthy of the sports pages, or 1,000 sparkline statistical graphics showing 500,000 numbers. *That one piece of paper shows the content-equivalent of 50 to 250 typical PP slides.* Thoughtful handouts at your talk demonstrate to the audience that you are responsible and seek to leave permanent traces and have consequences. *There is also a chance that the act of writing sentences and preparing a technical report will make for a smarter report,* an opportunity unavailable to those preparing PP slides.

Serious presentations might well begin with a concise briefing paper or technical report (the 4-pager) that everyone reads (people can read 3 or 4 times faster than presenters can talk). Following the reading period, the presenter might provide a guided analysis of the briefing paper and then encourage and perhaps lead a discussion of the material at hand.

*Consuming Presentations*

OUR evidence concerning PP's performance is relevant only to serious presentations, where the audience needs (1) to understand something, (2) to assess the credibility of the presenter. For non-serious pitches and meetings, the PP cognitive style may not matter all that much. Rather than providing information, *PowerPoint allows speakers to pretend that they are giving a real talk, and audiences to pretend that they are listening.* This prankish conspiracy against evidence and thought should provoke the question, *Why are we having this meeting?*

Consumers of presentations might well be skeptical of speakers who rely on PowerPoint's cognitive style. It is possible that these speakers are not evidence-oriented, and are serving up some PP Phluff to mask their lousy content, just as this massive tendentious pedestal in Budapest once served up Stalin-cult propaganda to orderly followers feigning attention.

Military parade, Stalin Square, Budapest, April 4, 1956. Photograph by AP/Wide World Photos.

"The Leonardo da Vinci of data" *The New York Times*

Edward Tufte has written seven books, including *Visual Explanations, Envisioning Information, The Visual Display of Quantitative Information, Data Analysis for Politics and Policy, Political Control of the Economy,* and *Size and Democracy* (with Robert A. Dahl). He writes, designs, and self-publishes his books on analytical design, which have received 40 awards for content and design. He is Professor Emeritus at Yale University, where he taught courses in statistical evidence, analytical design, and interface design. His current work includes landscape sculpture, teaching, and analytical design.

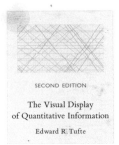

## THE VISUAL DISPLAY OF QUANTITATIVE INFORMATION   Second Edition

"One of the best books you'll ever see." DATAMATION   "A tour de force." JOHN W. TUKEY   "Best 100 nonfiction books of the 20th century." AMAZON.COM   "A classic reference. The overall intention and power of the book is stunning." OPTICAL ENGINEERING   "A visual Strunk and White." THE BOSTON GLOBE   "A beautiful, brilliant book." AMERICAN MATHEMATICAL MONTHLY   "A fascinating book, compulsory reading." NATURE   "Original, beautifully presented, sharp and learned, this book is a work of art. The art here is cognitive art, the graphic display of relations and empirical data, now an indispensable tool of science and engineering." SCIENTIFIC AMERICAN   $40 postpaid

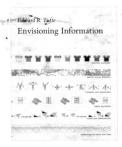

## ENVISIONING INFORMATION

"A remarkable range of examples for the idea of visual thinking with beautifully printed pages. A real treat for all who reason and learn by means of images." RUDOLPH ARNHEIM   "Buy this book. Keep it with the few others you have that you'll pass on to the next generation. Tufte is promoting a new standard of visual literacy. No other book has been so highly recommended to us by so many varieties of professionals — architects, teachers, technicians, hackers, and artists." WHOLE EARTH REVIEW   "Brilliant work on the best means of displaying information." SCI-TECH BOOK NEWS   "An incredibly beautiful, true, refined, and luscious book." DENISE SCOTT BROWN and ROBERT VENTURI   $48 postpaid

## VISUAL EXPLANATIONS: IMAGES AND QUANTITIES, EVIDENCE AND NARRATIVE

"By contents alone, this is easily one of the finest books of our time, but even more astonishing is the quality of every aspect of its production: text, illustrations, typography, page layout, paper and printing." BALLAST QUARTERLY   "This is the third in a series of beautifully produced books about the graphical display of data. Few books have been as widely acclaimed by so many readers working in as many fields as these have." JOURNAL OF THE AMERICAN MEDICAL ASSOCIATION   "The diversity of examples is awesome, a book is of the highest quality." JOURNAL OF THE AMERICAN STATISTICAL ASSOCIATION   "If this book were a house, it would have been designed by Frank Lloyd Wright." ONLINE   $45 postpaid

## BEAUTIFUL EVIDENCE

To be published in Spring 2006.

Fundamental Principles of Analytical Design   Sparklines: Intense, Simple, Word-Sized Graphics   Mapped Pictures: Images as Explanations and Evidence   Galileo's Evidence   Words, Numbers, Images—Together   Corruption in Evidence Presentations   The Cognitive Style of PowerPoint   The Sculptural Pedestal

Edward Tufte teaches a one-day course 'Presenting Data and Information,' which is offered in many cities; go to our website for more information. Order the books directly from Graphics Press at our website, or by phone, fax, mail.

GRAPHICS PRESS LLC   P. O. BOX 430   CHESHIRE, CT 06410   800 822-2454
FAX 203 272-8600   www.edwardtufte.com

ISBN 0-9613921-6-9